T0366296

Jottings

Jottings

The stories gathered in life's travels
By Walter Gerald (Jerry) Moon

Memories from a Lifetime of Love

iUniverse, Inc.
Bloomington

Jottings
Memories from a Lifetime of Love

Copyright © 2013 by Walter Gerald (Jerry) Moon .

All rights reserved. No part of this book may be used or reproduced by any means, graphic, electronic, or mechanical, including photocopying, recording, taping or by any information storage retrieval system without the written permission of the publisher except in the case of brief quotations embodied in critical articles and reviews.

iUniverse books may be ordered through booksellers or by contacting:

iUniverse
1663 Liberty Drive
Bloomington, IN 47403
www.iuniverse.com
1-800-Authors (1-800-288-4677)

Because of the dynamic nature of the Internet, any web addresses or links contained in this book may have changed since publication and may no longer be valid. The views expressed in this work are solely those of the author and do not necessarily reflect the views of the publisher, and the publisher hereby disclaims any responsibility for them.

Any people depicted in stock imagery provided by Thinkstock are models, and such images are being used for illustrative purposes only.
Certain stock imagery © Thinkstock.

ISBN: 978-1-4759-8283-1 (sc)
ISBN: 978-1-4759-8284-8 (ebk)

Library of Congress Control Number: 2013905654

Printed in the United States of America

iUniverse rev. date: 04/08/2013

Contents

Biographical . . . W.G. Moon

I find great pleasure in sharing my thoughts and joys by writing poetry. It gives a shorthand way to express the abundant feelings and thoughts of my life's walk. I am aware of the blessings of a wife and family who love me, and have made me rich in the important ways. I write as though I am summarizing the "secrets" of my living and of my values that I'd want others to discover about me. We really do harvest the seeds we sow in life. The future poem is always right there on the doorstep of living an active life, and expressing those words is so fulfilling.

WGM 2/1/2007

Dedicated to Carol, wife of 54 wonderful years of love and support.
I'll love you to eternity. Carol Z. Moon was born Feb 6, 1939; died November 17, 2012.

Foreword

This compilation of my poems from the Memories of a Lifetime of Love is offered for your pleasure and interest. None of this could have been possible without the patience, endurance and support of those who have been the subjects of my thoughts.

I thank you all for inspiring wonderful images of living extraordinary lives worthy of remembering so sweetly. As my poems reflect, you've made my life a fulfilling and worthwhile journey . . . worthy of collecting in my journal which I simply label as "Jottings".

Most assuredly, the foundation for all the feelings, utterances and reflections contained herein was facilitated by my lifetime mate and lover, for no one could ever release oneself to the "theatre of the mind", freely and wholly, without the blessing of a secure contentment which she has provided. When we are able to feel that we are worthy and appreciated we can do and visualize Extraordinary things! She's forever supported and encouraged me . . . our sons, and their families and close friends. our focus has always been on attending to the needs of our immediate family and extended family of nieces, cousins, close friends as our most important priorities in life.

I hope that my words reflect the honest feeling of the love blessings I've been privileged to receive in my walk; and most assuredly the blessing of having extraordinary talented and nurturing parents who energized the enthusiasm to strive for all that one can be. They led me to my faith in an awesome God and his creations everywhere.

Now, come join me in the "Theatre" as I share the produce of years of my personal "Jottings"

Preface

*Memories from a lifetime of love
the poetry and writings of Walter G. Moon*

The enclosed are random attempts to put down some of the poetry and writings I have felt about people, things, places and events. In so doing I hope to share these memories with anyone who reads . . . and to give myself the pleasure of returning to "the theater of my mind" where I might enjoy them again.

In my mind, a man is twice blessed if he <u>first</u> has the good fortune to see the beauty in life, and <u>second</u> has the reverence and good manners to return to say "thank you" once the glitter of the first instance has passed.

I am grateful for the parents whose initial guidance directed me to see love and optimism in my outlook. Their romanticism has definitely inspired me; and I am Thankful to God for having provided the perfect soul-mate for all my adult adventures. The lifetime of love we have shared . . . and the significant chance to know that I am secure in my manhood, has made it possible for me to better see and understand myself - my successes, my trials, my highs and my lows.

Finally, as a father, I have grown to better understand myself as a son . . . and now, as a father-in love to three wonderful daughters . . . and as grandfather to the most special little people any human could ever wish for . . . I feel free to share my journey openly and freely.

Alone In a Big City

There's times I like to be alone
but it's mostly in the woods.
To be alone in a big city is
so depressing.

It's like the feeling you get
when everyone knows the game -
except you . . .
and you're the one "out in left field".

Everyone else seems so
involved
in what they're doing.
They seem like it's all so much fun
but, I wonder if they really know where they're going.

I like the adventure of seeing new cities
and new places, but its strange that
though I yearn to be there, its not long before
I can't wait to get back home . . . where sanity is.

It's a paradox - at first it seems like such fun -
then it turns to boredom . . . or
at least a yearning for all I've already got.
Love, caring, purpose.

My mind drifts to there - - - when I'm alone

W G Moon, September, 1980 NYC

Appreciation

The difference between me and many folks I know is
that I have so much to be thankful for.
I've got friends like you to share with.
I've got a head full of memories -
about how great each and every day has truly been.

I love the way you laugh.
I love the way you listen.
I love the many small ways you say - - -
"man, you're a somebody worth knowing;
You are a character I can identify with . . .
even if we don't agree on every matter."

You know, I used to feel like many others who - - -
take it all in, but never stop to savor the experience -
something like the way kids
are prone to gulp down their meals,
because they want to get out to play ball.

But one day it hit me.
Suppose this was to be my last day on earth.
Would I regret that I let you go off thinking -
that I didn't accept you unconditionally for what you are ?
What a bummer that would be !

I decided right then, to make each and every day count . . .
to tell you I love you ;
and that whatever ways you did things was alright with me;
and if we come to different conclusions, that's O.K. too . . .
as long as we did it in love.

What's <u>really important</u> is that you get to know
that whatever you are; and
whatever you want to do, is O.K. with me -
because I really love you - the person . . .
even if I don't always love the action.

Maybe that's a different approach to life than others;
but it's an honest attempt to acknowledge that -
God has filled my life so abundantly that I must trust.
Through Christ, I've come to accept my life
as an active expression of His generous handiwork.

Yes, I'm different
because I appreciate that
though you're reading these words,
you're giving me the chance to share myself with you . . .
and, in a sense, to live beyond this time here.

And if perchance that - in any small way -
my life has touched somebody in a positive way . . .
then, I've really been a true son of God;
and my life has meant something even bigger than me.
Now, that's really something to appreciate.

W.G. Moon
January 12, 1982

To my loving sons, my dearest wife . . . and to you who know me by what my life -and my statement- has been.

Art is . . .

A line, a dash, a well placed splash of color
to suggest something well stored in our memory;
A twist of rope, or a rounded circle meeting a
perpendicular angle of our youth
where all is stored for a reunion of glee.

A place somewhere in mid air
which only we recognize as valid—
but everyone confirms it's theirs too when they
See it in your expression.

It's an urge . . . a necessity, put into form
in a very special way that only you can respond to at this moment,
in all its expressions, it is a way to let the "genie" out
to celebrate its' mood—

experience the sense of a particular joy inside -
the feeling of love, and life discovery ; and excitement
that's been waiting—pent up-
by life's many diversions.

It's the thing we knew at one time, but somehow lost
as we moved on in our life travels—
when in child-like glee we made our first mark on paper,
and heard the joy it gained from the guttural sounds of our mothers.

Art is the vehicle to take us by the potholes
of our own life adventure.
It restores our vision of the possibilities we've known,
And the adventures we've lost contact with.

WGM in Paris France
September 21, 1989

Beckoning

I listened until I could stand it no more.
The pain of staying outside it all was
just too much to bear,
so I did it !

I joined the little group of singers.
They were strangers,
but the music soon took care of that,
and they welcomed me.

I felt a tingly feeling all over
as she struck those golden chords.
Her fingers moved with grace and style,
and it was beautiful.

Oh how I love the song -
does it have to stop ?
I could stay all night, and enjoy the ecstacy.
Just one more please.

I felt so high -
as though time had stopped,
and I, suspended in mid air -
I felt a warm kind of glow, a cozy buzz.

Later, as the hour closed,
and my new friends satisfied their yearning,
it was over.
To me the time had passed in a second.

We all "split" -
and though I never spoke to her - I loved her,
for the beautiful feast
and for having brought us together for that magic moment.
W.G. moon, November, 1980, Rensselaerville, N.Y.

Scott, Jeff and Jay together

Just Being There

When the world hands you a "bummer"
and you feel like you could cry.
It's a fortunate person who has
loved ones to turn to.

Fortunate is the guy -or gal-
who can turn inward for help'
knowing, really knowing, someone will care . . .
someone who'll listen with loving ears . . .
someone who'll actually feel the pain with you.

The greatest act of love - is sharing ;
to really empathize because you know
how it feels to "be there";
to "share the load".

I love you so much because
You're there for me when I need you;
and I love you because you're there ---
for each other too !
Now, that's real family for you.

The nicest things you could ever give your Mom and Me,
is to be aware that you are loved <u>so much</u>
you can afford to give something of yourself away . . .
to each other . . . to other dear souls in need -
wherever you find them.

When one brother reaches out to the other,
we feel your reflected warmth.
Like saying -to us - that you heard the penultimate line
in this act of living we've been playing out.

How sweet a prize - to see that love flows
through this body of close kinship.
Miles cannot stop those urges,
nor can time ever erase the feeling of confirmation -
when all those joined through the golden chain that
binds our heartstrings - seek to smother your pain.

Each of you "hunks" look so beautiful to us -
the glow of the strength born through this special unity.
It surpasses mere logic . . . a powerful force !
Always keep that power working for you, dear ones,
no matter where you are ___

Yes, I can be happy -
because you've shown through your living . . . and loving,
that no matter where you are,
<u>you can always be there for each other.</u>

I love you, dear ones,
just as you have loved today !

W.G. Moon
November, 1984

*Inspired by the way everyone . . . Jay, Pam, Ann, Jeff . . . reached out to Scott when he
suffered the predictable, but nonetheless painful and real, trauma of breaking up with
Lois. Oh, those terrible teens --- we all knew them !*

*Jay, with Pam's help and understanding, drove up from Blacksburg
"to be there". Pam wrote from her heart. Ann came by . . . and Jeff "reached out" from
across the seas—from
Thailand -- where he was an AFS student at the time.*

BIG BRO, BIG SIS

Marie and Bob are the best sort of friends -
no demands, no posturing, no pressure . . .
They're just there !
There's something comforting about them.

Like you feel about your family.
You never think about loving them;
but then you can't think about a single time
when you didn't just love them either.
They're the best sort of example;
the way that Marie rules Bob while

all the time pretending that he's in charge.
Bob just lets out that silly grin of his
and shrugs like he's saying
"whatever will be will be".
But I ask you, what's the diff anyway?
What works, works . . . and they sure make it work !

Bob's such a flirt. He's always been that way.
Marie seems to prod him on as though she knows
that there's a little elf inside that keeps him growing younger
all the time . . .
"from two to toothless" she says.
Now who could resist that kind of huggy bear love ?

Marie's alive with life and caring for so many others,
she's got no time for phonies.
We've known her for many years as the one who's
always there for you . . . your own big sister
who listens in a way that says "the world has stopped,
and you are the only important person right now."

I love that little twinkle in her eye that says "I love you";
and love she does in so many ways.
She drives Carol into madness,
pushing her to a flea market frenzy.
You'd think she could jump a big building in a single bound
when she's behind the scheme.

Bob and Marie bring back so many warm memories
every time they show up;
and you'll just never know where they might be.
They've shared so many personal times with us
we never stop re-living those scenes;
and who wants to ever stop?

We've played together, prayed together and made life together
. . . so much of what life is all about;
the kind of elegant experience that speaks so boldly
about their Christian walk.
If you saw people so filled with the abundance of life,
wouldn't you want to know how they did it ?

A model of all that God promised the faithful:
they have laughs, they have enough to eat,
they have all they need to make life flow;
and they have the abundance of good friends
and family who love them.
What more could a body need?

But on top of all that
they've got the precious gift of each other,
and a family who loves them . . . and who
reflect the fruits of a special kind of nurturing.
No words or explanation needed.
And finally, but certainly not least,

they've got us ; the many people
whose lives they've touched in many ways . . .
Big Bro, big Sis ; we wish you wealth in love
forever and ever !

W.G. Moon
February, 1987

This was inspired by a surprise visit Marie and Bob made to celebrate Carol's 1987 birthday, shared with Harland and Jill Williams. Marie and Bob are family, whose presence reeks of the love we have shared for many years, and the kind of love these two "lovebirds" shed wherever they go; and since the timing was the Valentine season, I was inspired to send this note to them.

Broke—So Fix it

God Hears
He hears the inner voice of His child—
Who cries out in desperate need:
A child who seeks just to touch His gown.

A simple act-
But one that reveals a sincere and trusting
Search for balance and stability in a life buffeted by world troubles-
A "home base" from all that threatens us.

When we can trust Him-
I mean, really trust Him;
And put all our hopes and inner desires in His hands;
He will deliver us from all evil.

God clearly promised—
That if we present our worries and troubles to His son, Jesus Christ.
Our earnest prayers for His help will be heard.
He will lift our problems from us—to Him with simple Grace.

He delivers !
But we must ask;
And we must trust that He will lift our hurt.
God didn't lie, nor will He ever lie to those He loves so dearly.

WGM November 2008

Hear the Bugle

My friend Roland is a rather special guy.
He's not at all like the typical sort you might expect to meet . . .
but you could meet him when you least expect it.
He loves people who are alive with thought . . .
and he seeks out those kind -
to make a very special kind of friendship with them.

Now, don't get me wrong:
Roland's not idle, or anything like that; quite the contrary.
He's a busy sort; always yearning to know more . . .
about himself, and his fellow creatures.
He really gets turned on about subjects dealing with spiritual and aesthetic achievements.

He seldom dwells on sports and such;
he has a deep interest in family . . . especially those he's cared for and watched over,
during many "growth years".
We find times to "retreat" together.
Nothing fancy, but somewhere we can talk, and talk, and talk.
We discover we've lost all track of time !

We "let it all roll out".
Practically no subject, or thought, is spared;
even if it's the kind of thing where you have to say it "straight out" . . .
knowing it will land gently, but firmly . . .
because the trust we've built is a caring concern
without all the accouterments that usually cloud most conversations.

Roland is a strange "bird".
He's got that rakish look that becomes the actor that he is.
Did you know that he's played in John Water's movies,
and acted in little theater for years?
I wonder what his Mother would have said if she saw
one of those Water's "flicks" . . .
especially the parts with Divine.

I know that his daughter, Lois, accidentally saw one at college
one year, and was aghast !
Roland does this and that.
Nothing escapes his interest . . . even in passing.
One time he's off on some worthwhile mission
to serve the neglected, or deprived.

Another time he's "soaring with the masters" in a great book.
God bless him !
Roland doesn't always stop with his own resources.
If you aren't careful, you'll find yourself involved
in one of his adventures.
He loves life so . . . and he's such an unselfish guy.

Once he even gave me a plaque that said . . .
"to a real true friend".
I've received a lot of awards in my lifetime,
but I never got one bettern' that !
Once, no twice, I found myself giving a speech I never volunteered for . . .

on "the Magic Power of Self Image Psychology" -
to a group of parents without partners.
One woman said, she wished she could give that message
to all high school teenagers . . .
to make them feel more positive about themselves.
Leah's remark was "humbug! . . . more un necessary garbage."

As for me, and my performance there . . .
I don't even know how I ever got there;
but I saw Roland with "a smoking gun".
He gives me all sorts of credit for being much better than I am.
He recently said - about a prior time in his life -
that he couldn't have made it, if we hadn't had our "talks".

That's the nicest thing anyone, other than Carol,
ever said to me.
I only wish I felt I really was so worthy ___
but that's the best thing about really close friends -
You are always special -
to them !

But Roland advises me too.
I can see him now with that uplifted brow . . .
his bushy brows make him look a wee bit wild, as he does that;
and when he says "now, let me just tell you something
Mr Moon",
I know I'm in for his usual "shot" at me.

His lectures usually go directly to the same theme . . .
that I've spent entirely too much of myself -
time, energy, and my caring - on others . . .
"and it's high time you should spend more time on
yourself, and your needs ".
He means well . . . and he usually throws in a few "ah,ah, ahs" -
He's well known for these.

We had a talk just recently.
I told him that I appreciate what he was saying;
but that he was missing the significance
of a particular aspect of our relationship . . .
I should clarify this, lest he overlook my motive.
This factor probably drew our friendship in the first place.

That is that life is just like a great journey;
that the real joy is in the travel, not the arriving;
and in traveling forward into uncharted dimensions,
one must be prepared to expose themself -
not just sit by --- and watch.
I claim that each day is a smorgasbord of OPPORTUNITY . . .

Some adventures are easy; others are hard ___
but yet, in retrospect,
it's the hard ones that seem the sweetest.
That's the point I wanted to tell him.
To him it seemed like my pace was dangerous . . .
and perhaps it would be to anyone else who places themselves
at stress during strenuous activity.

But me, I can't possibly stop.
I hear the bugle, and I must go ___
for one more great adventure !
But I think he knows, as I do,
that we'd <u>both</u> wish to go on, and on . . .
reaching, always reaching --- for our fellows hand . . .

because somehow in loving so much,
to care so immediately,
we are compelled to do what must be done.
Timing is so important . . .
no one else seems to notice, or to care.
Roland, my friend, you're just like that too.

Can't you see it?
That's why we speak so clearly.
It's not just the words; they're such an awkward media . . .
we've been communicating in a different dimension.
We've engaged in extra sensory transmission
where the thrill of the absolute truths ---

of revelations we've discovered . . . are confirmed.
Think about this -
If life were a theater, and we were called out
to account for all the roles we've played,
there'd be many a soul we'd rescued . . .
as we always said "many a twig we'd broken" - - -

to show the way to those who follow;
and stripping away the age,
religious and cultural differences between us . . .
we'd be dammed close to twins !

W.G. Moon
January, 1987

Inspired by the incessant and continuous praises of a well intentioned friend. Roland, the actor . . . the friend for over thirty years now . . . deserves to know that his gift of his life to many others was not in vain.

I Love Camping OUT

I love camping out;
It makes a human being out of me again.
When the pressures of business and the struggle
of it all has done its worst -
to hitch up, and hit the highway,
seems to bring a release of all those tensions -
like saying, "aw forget it; leave it for the second shift."

Everyone senses it - like drifting upward
over it all _ _ _ not caring if it ever ends.
I just want to go, and don't particularly care where that is
except that it should be somewhere with no hassles.

Isn't it interesting that when you get there
you're just beginning a new adventure.
Who cares what your "rig" looks like -
as long as it keeps out the weather.
Just give me a nice piece of shady real estate
where cool breezes blow each night within shootin' distance
of new sights . . .

Give me a fire to watch, and new stars to see,
and I'll be happy.
If perchance I find someone to sing with,
that's all the better,
but I'll be satisfied
with whatever I find.

There's no status here.
Everyone shares equally without uniforms or masks.
The bath house is alive with talk of past camp spots . . .
of where you're going and where you've been;
but most of all how great we all feel
to be here . . . together !

Yes, that's it - together.
Togetherness is what we've got that feels so good.
It's a place where everyone fits in and does their bit.
From tending fire, to doing the dishes, we all help.

People who don't have time to say "hello" back home
find time to sit and chat -
not really about anything important;
but what's wrong with that ?

I just like you; I like this place;
I just like this feeling ---
the smells, the lights, and the noises
of people being happy together.

There's something about camping
that brings out the best in people.
Where even strangers stop by to say "how do",
where no one locks their door and hides their things.
The only time I've been robbed was by a hungry Racoon
in search of sustenance.
I didn't mind.

The airs so fresh it swells the nostrils.
It relaxes the psyche in all God's creatures . . .
restoring them to wholeness.
Then comes the time for gathering addresses,
along with the pledge to "share again".
Camping . . . I love it !

W.G. Moon
September,1980

Charette, Charette

That's what the students of the Art Academy in Paris call out.
Their goal is to receive input and criticism for their freshly painted work.
They hold their painting high, inviting all comments from the gathered peers . . .
While their palate and canvas is still wet enough to accommodate change.

They invite diverse views, and reflection of solicited emotion—from all,
As they strive for completion of the object reflecting their final expression.
For example, if the subject is love, one tends to seek yellow, pale purple
Blue and green and red.

For the emotion of hate or fear, one tends toward black, dark brown, or gray.
Meanwhile the artist is compelled to express the perfect mood and shape—
Selection of their right tone and shade enables the artist to catch the perfect mood.
Everyone's input is considered; but the final decisions are the artist's domain.

An unobserved smudge; a misdirected stroke; or an over exaggerated dot;
Or understated tone or shade can spoil what might have been a masterpiece.
Equally so, a missed opportunity for an appropriate object in the distant landscape
Can change the opportunity to convey something the viewer may connect with.

It seems strange, to me, that if our life is to be our own personal masterpiece—
Why then do we resist the appropriate council of qualified peers-
Wouldn't it seem that much is to be gained by the very same cited process-
That we might be better off seeking opinion while our "masterpiece" is still wet?

Charette! Charette!

November 14, 2006
W.G. Moon

Carol, who made it all worthwhile

DADDY DAY 1996

You're the girl who made me a daddy.
I couldn't have done it myself.
When I reflect on all the joy you've brought me,
being made a daddy is just a part --

but for me -- and better yet us,
being made a daddy
is one of the most important and special projects
we ever did together.

Some people are lucky in love.
Few are lucky in life, as we are.
We owe a lot to each other, lest we e're forget -
but the lives we grew from love we dared

has been beyond anything anyone could guess
when we said "until death will we part."
When we kids said we'd raise a family -
and raise them well -

We were starry-eyed and unsure
just like many others. But somehow we learned,
that there are special parts to give of each of us
- mommy and daddy - that makes the lessons whole.
In looking back now at the years and years
of all those daddy days, I see how blessed I am,
that God gave me that special you,
and because of you, I am a daddy;

and because of that special you, and me,
the "little people" that now go toward paths we've opened,
are good - clean - honest striving folk - -
grateful for their roots and the image of home
where Mom and Dad will forever reside.

W.G. Moon
June, 1996

You're a Special Deal

You're a special deal, that's what you are.
I'm such a proud, proud pa pa.
Who'd ever believe that the "snip" we raised,
is now a Phi Beta Kap-pa.

But what's there in being a PBK;
such a man - could there be better ?
Can you imagine the thrill - the joy Mom had
the day you brought home the letter.

To be the best is grand to be sure;
but that's not all that's important.
It's you the guy, the man you've become,
the quality of your fine deportment.

We're so happy to say this fine day in May,
in the year of nineteen and eighty one,
that we're so proud, to say out loud,
that you're a star, a Moon, and our son !

W.G. Moon
May, 1981

Dedicated to our son Jeffrey on his occasion of his induction into Phi Beta Kappa

The Dealer's Hand

The Great Dealer dealt the hand,
and I drew it _
as I looked at it I knew at once
it was THE HAND I dreaded;
but that's the game _ _ _
I must play it out.

"CA" is what the Doctor told me . . .
"that lump must come out . . . and maybe more."
The words cut through me.
My soul moaned . . .
Are you sure . . . it's MY turn ?
I must play it out.

I want to run, and hide _ _ _
give it to someone else !
I don't even like the sound of it -
words like "lump-ec-tomy" and "radical",
they shake me to my soul.

Thoughts of resulting disfigurement -
of the nasty things that scalpel might do
run swiftly through my mind.
The unsaid words, the whispers . . .
"she lost her breast to cancer" -
stop - I can't stand this !

But what choice do I have ?
The hand's been dealt, and . . .
I can't deny what <u>must</u> be done.
"What God delivers, God can take away".
These are the words of comfort I'll strive for -
to keep me on solid ground.

As I "settle in" with the thought of this
inevitable thing _ _ _
My mind reaches toward my support.
Oh how I need them now . . . of all times.
God bring them near, and
let me clutch them.

If I've got to do this,
and as surely as I wish I didn't have to
I know I must . . .
God give me the strength - and faith -
to bring me through it

Inspired by news that my mother is scheduled for surgery for a lump.

Depression

Depression is a thief.
It steals your spirit when you least expect it.
It creeps in when you have doubts about yourself,
and how you're doing.
It somehow knows just how and where to get you -
then zing ! there it is _ _ _ depression.

Depression is nothing at all.
You can't see it.
You can't touch it; but
it feeds on the best you have to give.
It tries to get you when you're alone and most vulnerable.
It knows just how, and when, to make you feel just plain awful.

Depression says "you'll never do it",
why bother to even try;
and if you're not extra careful it'll even make you cry.
It's like a cloud that overtakes you
when you're reaching for the sky -
or like more rain drops when you're feeling kinda blue.

But there's a formula to fight depression
if you ever really dare.
It's the time to love somebody, just to show you really care.
You'll be surprised to see it working,
when you give it just a chance.
Just give an act of kindness. Try to take a stance.

There's something about making that investment
that seems to do the trick.
It's the very kind of medicine that makes your clock
regain it's tick.
When you focus on some other, and you're friends fill up the room
___ the feeling overtakes you, and drives away the gloom.

It starts out ever so slowly, as you open up the door.
It pays to help somebody, as you come up from the floor.
The dividends are terrific -
if you trust yourself to give.
It'll kick the low, and lift you high . . .
It gives reason - the purpose for which to live.

You get so much back when you "go the extra mile";
so go ahead and try it;
And if you fall, or need support, don't even dare deny it.
Just get up again, and love some more; Just try a little harder.
For life's worth the living, through the wondrous joy of giving -each step it gets better.

Depression - get away !
and let's get on with living.

W.G. Moon
August, 1984

THE DIRTY JOB

There's no way you could pay me enough to do the job that I see must be done.
There's simply not enough money in the world to make one strive so hard.

Some would see the mountain of work that must be done and say,
"I'll do my fair share, but no more "!
Others would say "it just can't be done without more help";
But me, I'm inspired by the goal that draws me ever deeper.

I see something in it all that you might not see.
I see the wagon tracks through unblazed trails . . .
the campfires on the rim of uncharted hills.

I have a vision of something worth the striving for,
with all you've got to give.
I don't care what it costs, it simply must be done,
for the sake of those who follow.

The very audacity of a man, or woman, who really thinks they can make a difference . . .
to make things better because of their efforts.
It's an obsession in my genes.
My kin have always been in there . . . at the edge of progress . . . from the beginning of
civilized time.

God is my master; but love is my engine.

The money, well that's only stepping stones,
to let me trod this adventurous path.
I enjoy the privilege . . . to pay back some of the blessings
of an abundant life that God has delivered me.

An abundance that overflows!

The world is my "fruitcake" as long as God's children suffer;
As long as there are undeveloped things that need attention;
God gave me the talent, the strength, and the love to go there.

There's no way you could pay me to do what God wants done;
But there's no way you could stop me either!

W.G. Moon
January, 1996

Picture of Walter M. Moon

Echoes of My Father's Love

Those echoes rebound
From the utterances of your soul
I still hear their tug
Yet today.

From the days I recall
When but I was a lad
You bathed me in their strains
so clear.

My head hears your voice . . .
tunes so fine and sweet -
of love, and home and family . . .
of how our God still reigns supreme . . .

In our car as we traveled,
wherever our campfires,
or family times,
as you sang those songs in church.

I hear you now
Even more than before before;
my soul feels the tug of your hand,
your music still lives in my heart.

W.G. Moon
November 2003

Inspired by thoughts of the wonderful treat I was fortunate to have all my life . . .a father and mother who sang incessantly wherever we were. Songs of old, and songs of present and past times. Now that they are both gone I realize that they were teaching me about values amidst our history. My dad was the music man deluxe, and now sings a lead part in God's celestial choir with my mother's alto voice right behind.

Emptiness

There are times when even I feel just plain empty -
as though someone pulled the plug on everything I stand for.

Why, I ask is it so darned important to please ?
But that's what bothers me.
I tried to share important things,
and something you said, or didn't say out loud,
made me feel so small.

I'll bounce back - to see things better tomorrow;
but for now, it hurts !

You have your life, and I have mine. I expect that.
But what gets to me is a feeling - I know it's not real-
but it feels real just the same . . . that your silence conveys.
It tells me that you disapprove,
and that in my eagerness to talk, I hadn't listened.

But, you know what ?
You never shared what you were thinking _ _ _
only that special bit of silence.

Oh how I hate to feel this way !

W.G. Moon
July, 1981

to Jeff, whose searching for his own kind of inner peace often leaves me feeling helpless; yet whose travels and questions reflect the same kind of struggle we all go through, to some extent. My heart understands what my words sometime fall short of meeting.

It's strange how, as a parent, we wish we could save all the struggle and pain ___ yet we know that every man must be left to find his own way. I'm more aware than ever now, that it takes real courage to love hopefully.

Picture of Jerry on way to Africa

Picture of Carol on way to Africa

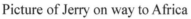

THE WAY I FELT TODAY

I wish that I could always feel,
the way I felt today;
The peaceful buzz, the lilting chord,
the spot along some way.

The heart is meant for singing;
the soul; rests in sweet refrain;
the friends they are at parting;
Can you feel the sweet old pain ?

For parting is full of sweetness;
the goodbyes are all the same.
The tears you choke back fainting,
that you'll see them soon again.

For you gave yourself so completely,
without price or 'ere regret;
But the way we felt today dear;
We never will forget.

Yes parting brings its' sadness,
but there's ne're room left to fret;
'cause the thoughts you feel,
are the one's you'll keep - -
and life's not over yet!

It's the tinge of lasting sadness,
for the one's you've met and touched;
that gives you life and full reward,
for the memories you loved so much.

But the best of all the goodness,
about what we've shared along life's way,
is the fact, my dear, that you were there,
to share the way I felt today.

W.G. Moon
September, 1994
Vancouver, Canada

Sittin' Round My Franklin'

Snow flake on the window,
Scottie's on the run,
to gather in the fuel
for ol' Franklin'.

There's something special that happens
when ol' Franklin starts "his thing".
He sets the stage for all kinds
of times.

For reading and relaxing,
for singing and "plucking",
or just sharing what you feel
with loved ones.

It's so cozy there,
like being held close as a peg in a shore place.
I heightens your senses, and your ability to listen
. . . sittin' 'round my Franklin'.

W.G. Moon
November 1980

(Scott was age 14 when he inspired this)

Giving a Part of Yourself Away

There's something special in the way you act;
that quiet way you have of watching . . .
and then you move your hand, and wow !
All sorts of magic flows out.

I've seen you do it time and time again;
As if you had planned it all before . . .
tried it as a dress rehearsal;
and I'm simply awed by that special gift of yours.

When I try it I see so many lines and details;
but you, you have a talent for abstraction
that goes right to the heart of your subject -
and lifts out the most significant !

You lift the soul of the thing,
and put it right there - - -
a real masterpiece, as I see it.
But what do you do?

You rip it off the easel,
and start another . . .
like a rich man
gives away his pennies.

I just don't know how you can do it;
I'd be so proud, I'd want to show everyone.
"Look, see what I've accomplished."
But you ? you <u>appear</u> to never look back . . .

but I caught you!
I saw that look out of the corner of your eye.
You cared more about what your gift <u>did</u> to the one
who received it, than whether it was good art or not.

I caught that little "I love you" you wrote there.
You can't fool me, Mr Artist. I see it all now !
All the time I thought you were giving away sketches,
you were really giving away a piece of yourself.

What a beautiful gift . . . you old faker !

W.G. Moon
April 30,1982

Inspired by Arnold Leiberman . . . an artist, observer,
philosopher - whose many pictures have brought so many smiles to the faces of those who
needed them most . . . and whose unselfish sharing, and unqualified friendship has left
the day a lot brighter.
Many years of drawing while "Jerry and the Moonshiners" played music.

Glasses and Keys

Isn't it funny how something as simple and routine as glasses and keys
Can suddenly, and unexpectedly, become so all- fired important!.
After all, they are just objects.

I just hate myself afterward for being so irritated and impatient-
Over nothing really important at all;
Yet I do it every time you ask to borrow my keys, or say "I can't find my glasses."

Of course, its always when time is important, or when we are late getting away.
There must be some rule in that, but I can't seem to work it out.
Again, the routine that upsets and unbalances my usual quiet, patient nature.

I always say . . . "if you'd just put them in one place, you'd know where they are,."
And then you just give that look ---
The one that says, "I just don't work like that" as though that makes it all right.

What is worse, for me, is when I go running around the house trying to find my own
glasses
And then find out that you've picked mine up.
We find that out after I say, "O.K., its see test time" ; and there they are in your pocket
book.

The keys are even worse for me.
After you borrow them, I've got to "hound you" to get them back—
That's not a part of your system either . . . oh, oh, another of those looks—

I try to tell myself that if that is all we have to "debate about", then our life's not too bad
---
But then the very next time we get ready to go out, it happens again !
And you guessed it . . .I'm in there again . . . and I get another of those looks.
;

W.G.Moon
November 10,2006

God's Love

(I've Got to Write Down Some Words of Love Tonight)

I've got to write down some words of love tonight
and post 'em on every door.
They'll have the sweet sweet smell of Jesus on earth,
with the spirit of the holy one.

I'll polish and hone till the message comes out,
write big on every page,
Cause He said . . . you gotta write down some words of love for me,
That's how the preacher gets paid!

When the chorus tries to add " hallelujah",
the saints will just say "amen"
and ah huh, ya know, we're ready to go
I'm ready where'er God sends.

I've got to write down some words of love tonight,
How else'll we know we've been saved?
It all begins with a few little words,
and a few steps . . . one, two and three

So I'll be busy tonight,
what a wonderful sight,
when I write down those words again
what He meant for you and for me

I'll travel this wide wide country, and write it on every tree;
I'll find the folks a hurtin' the most
and we'll sing out praise for the one who cares about me;
the Father, Son and Holy Ghost.

Oh, I've got to put down on paper what He told me to say,
I'll shout out His love on every page,
just what He meant for you and for me.
Shout "hooray", "hallelujah" what a blessing this is for me.

Oh I've got to write down some words 'bout the Fathers true love
He paid the price for you and me, now the bill has been paid,
the bill's been marked "paid in full
in the name of sweet Jesus, amen!

W.G. Moon, August 2000

Jerry, Scott and Chaska watching a kite

A Grandpa in Need of a Grandchild

I saw a white-haired couple on the beach today -
in typical beach attire -
he with faded green shorts - tan open necked tee shirt,
she in white hat - white - with white loose pants and visor.

He beaconed for her help . . . to launch their craft.
a kite - in triangle design- black & pink & purple & green.
Swish - up it went -first straight -then dip --
and off to the side - then straight upward --
to a resting spot above.

And she -- contented that she had done her job,
for the man - that for the moment - was a boy again --
did what every good beach loving partner would do -
she searched the edge of the turf for useless shells . . .

The kind you crave - in that moment of relaxed imagination -
then later in "the different world" --
where normal reference, rather than serendipity, takes over -
you wonder what to do with them.

He let his craft dive . . .
ever so close to the ground -
then wisk ---in a second it's up to a heavenly hole.
It's a game he's playing.

Like the one those gray pelicans play just beyond the shore
at wave top endings - there in a line -
like soldiers in a row; 4 - 5 - 6 in pure formation . . .
tickling the wave tops ---in search of prey.

As I watched the boy - man, and his helpful mate at play -
I couldn't help but utter . . . "tis a shame" -
"there's a grandpa in need of a grandchild to play with"
_ _ _ and my partner said . . . "aren't we all !"

W.G. Moon
July 15,1996
Nags Head N.C.

Eileen & Kathleen Lynch rubbing

Gravestone Rubbings

Hello my friend, my pal, my progenitor.
You're the one whose genes inspired my being.

Though I've only known about you through others,
I try to reach you by touching—
And through this action—
I hope to feel the history—
The honor,
The statement you made of your life.

Somehow, by rubbing
What is now a testament to your life—
I sense the testor,
Who for but a brief time so long ago-
Was given the privilege of action—
To choose a path well staked for me.

To be sure, I had choices and temptations,
As did you.
And this stone is but a small account
Of what you did.
But now I say "rest now in your peace"-
that the love that lived in you was good.

And was well invested.
Your produce was great—
As evidence that your just true value
Was more than just a stone Mason.
It is now we who must shoulder the legacy
we inherited.

To move on, and ever forward in our own time now,
To the benefit of those who follow us.

WGM 11/5/98

Inspired by a trip to North Carolina with my mother in the fall 1998. We stopped in
N.C. and Tenn to gather gravestone rubbings of the early great Lynch and Seabolt
pregenerators.

Johns Hopkins Hospital

Christ the healer statue, Hopkins

To Soothe Your Grieving Heart

I wish I had but the right words
to soothe your grieving heart
in desperate times like these one feels so alone;
and I so useless, to see a friend suffer so

But keep your eye to the East,
from where God comes in the early morn.
He is the rock, the comforter,
The one who cares and will show the way.

He promised to stay the path
midst all life's trials and snares.
Even in times where we feel most separated
from the joys we've known . . .

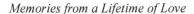

He's always there with hands outstretched.
He is the Alpha and Omega.
He will bring you home safely.
He promised . . . and God doesn't lie

W.G. Moon
September 18, 2000

To my friend Roland . . . whose heart ache's for his wife of many years . . . dying in a coma state . . .
Slowly, and without a sign of recognition. My heart goes out to him.

How Well Will You Know Me?

By my patient loving ways ? (I hope)
By my songs and poems about you whom I have loved so much? (I hope)
By the many times we talked; and shared the products of our memories;
The things we cared about? (I hope)

About the many ways I found you interesting? And the many things
You'd learned along the way that you thought I might like? (I hope)

About how much we shared common values; and the beauty you've seen through
Your sparkling green eyes from your ancient Norse DNA ancestry? (I hope)

My hope is that when you see your own family,
you'll see another glimpse of me; this regular guy who tried, and cared.

And think of what I said to you today . . .
How well will you know me when I'm gone?

W.G. Moon, July 7, 2011

Inspired by my thoughts of my wonderful family (wife; sons, daughters-in love, and grandchildren), as I was driving North to our "escape place" at Hedgesville, in the beautiful Shenandoah Mountains.

I Knew I loved you; and wanted you to be my life partner

I knew I loved you, the very first time I saw you at the "Hamilton Rec.".
We were so young . . . you were 14; I was a big 16.
So naive; yet so certain that everything would work out.

I still remember the day I proposed,
On my knees while parked at "our spot" at Lock Raven Dam . . .
Would you marry me?

The diamond in the ring I worked for by painting houses after work, at Ailsa Market
Was sooo small ; you could barely see it; But I was proud when you said "yes" . . .
In early 1956, as I headed off to College Park and the University of Maryland.

That seems so long ago now—but the memory of those times is still very clear to me.
It was later, in May 1958 that we "tied the knot" . . . and we gladly worked several jobs . . .
Looking towards my graduation in June 1960, when I could assume full responsibility for
our household. Jeff was there at my graduation . . . born November 1959.

We've been blessed that everything did work out for us . . . even when many around us drifted.
We've so many memories; so many nice stories to tell our children and grandchildren.
We've had many "mountain top experiences" . . . together . . . camping and enjoying with family.
Our three very unique and outstanding "only sons" have brought us and amazing life!

Who could ever have imagined when we first danced at the Hamilton Rec., or a "Ma Hogan's"?
Some might have said that we were really too young to know what love is. You were only 19.
I was three months shy of 21 . . . but, for me, I knew . . . and I'd do it all over again!

You are the core of my life . . . my very best and closest friend.
I'll love you into eternity.

Love always and forever,
Jerry
May 2012

If You Could But Imagine

If you could only imagine the truth
of what I say to you today,
You'd know that our love as we knew it back then
Is alive as it was that first day.

Years of adventures have come and gone,
And there's nothing we couldn't do;
And most of it now, looking backward
Is a victory shared with you.

I've often said "how is it,
that two young kids like we,
Ever found our way from there to here"
But we did it well, as all can see.

I couldn't begin to tell you
how much you've meant to me,
Or how much your constant council
Has balanced and guided me.

You said it too, and I thought—how sweet: how true
That we did it all together as our children steadily grew
And now we've got all worth having,
And savoring, it's true

If you can only imagine . . . my life so filled with you

WGM Feb 1, 2007

The Important Things

I met someone the other day who asked me to tell them
what I thought really important in my life.
I began by pouring out my feelings about love of home
and family, as my number one values;
how having been blessed with those who love me
has made it all possible.

To be sure, there were times where I tested that love -
by stretching a bit too far -
by failing to sense the opportunity to thank them.
But then, I'm human.

I turned to my need for social and professional expression.
I acknowledge that this drive for self esteem is strong,
but not so strong as to make me want to destroy others
in my wake.
But I do enjoy a challenge !

He then asked if I feared God, or death.
I said unequivocally "no" !
I love God, and God loves me;
and I am saved by His power
which has been promised.

I tried to say that my life has been full beyond my share;
that already I have lived more than those twice my age;
that if I were to die tonight
I'd want no man to feel sorrow for my passing.
Why ?

For I've lived in love, and have done my best -
the rest is up to God.
I am His creature,
His conduit for his worldly presence,
and I'll follow His bidding.

But as I looked into his eye,
I saw no understanding.
Though he asked, He really couldn't hear -
not because he didn't want to, but
because he really wasn't willing to make the step.

W.G. Moon
Rennsalerville, N.Y., November 1980

In the Pure Joy of the moment

Come walk with me again as we did in those cool, cool days of spring,
When our hearts were young, and even giddy, with the anticipation
That comes from discovery, and hopes and unfettered dreams to come.
Where the morning brings a new chance to be all that one could hope to be.

Smell the roses; see the fog lifting on that hillside in the distance-
And in this state of mind, there's nothing that stands between us and the choice of a path
of sweet tomorrows where we'll linger a bit
To savor the flavor of those shared thoughts and times.

I'll let you chase me around the house like a game of two young kids,
But now, as I've told our sons, I'll slow down a bit and let you catch me-
And in my arms I'll shower you with all the flowers and sweet words you so deserve, my
dear partner and lover for all those wonderful years.

I still believe in the responsible way that we choose to be hopeful, and happy,
We can set the stage—to be happy, and thus draw our contentment and joys-
Or to give in to the many tempting and petty short term side trails that lead one to
seemingly self- justified, but unfulfilling ends.

Our spring has led us wisely to the summer, fall, and even winter seasons—
One wonderful day at a time—
And now I can clearly see over the rise that all—good and testing—
Has led us safely on to good today's, and expectations of good tomorrows.

As we often say, we've been blessed to have many wonderful "magic moments" to carry us on—
Where what we see, and feel, is inspired by the pure joy of those wonderful moments together, linked as surely as a planned patchwork quilt of our lives.

Where our joy together has inspired those who follow,
To dare to be hopeful and joyful in their moments and trials—
And where the purposeful gathering of experiences of pure joy out weighs all the other things that get in the way of our chances at happiness

.

W. G. Moon
July 2006

INHERITANCE

I wish I had but a moment
To kiss your wrinkled brow
Once more.

To say I'll love you
To eternity - -
As I did in days before -

And now you're gone,
Sweet mother,
And eternity is hard to see -

But the love you've left
Behind you,
Is residing here in me.

Walter G. Moon
June 20, 2002

Eileen Moon's smiling eyes

Where's the Irish In Those Eyes ?

Seems to me that no matter what we do or say
there's no joy to be found _ anywhere.

It's though when the grave claimed him
you stopped your travel
to act, and wait for your turn . . .
Without any thought that others
take their que from you.

Such as what living is about.
The twinkle in those Irish eyes, that you are so noted for
has dimmed,
replaced by a stare that shows nothing but
emptiness . . .

And to recall the joys you had
of love, and joy and caring ---
things had by precious few in this life
seem now discarded for this lifeless act
you now display.

I know that he would be so sad to know
that what he built for you was not enough,
that all that love and joy had ensnared the one
who was the whole focus for his acts.
He loved you with every word and song.

You were the center of it all !!

Yet now, as I look upon your sweet face
the one who inspired such life in me . . .
Of art, of song of craft -
I ask myself, how could it be ? Was it all a lie?
And in this self-assured question is the challenge for us all --

Do we love so poorly
when those we leave behind are crippled by our passing?
Shouldn't we be judged by what we've left
as a legacy of our living
just as when we had that brief privilege of life ?

To you who I have loved take heed.
The lesson here is clear.
To me, the lesson I learned was this:
that all who have been given privilege
have a *responsibility* to pass it on.

Yes, even if you call it bravery,
or nobility ----
we must reflect the gratefulness *and gracefullness*
of a good life, well lived, in all we do.
Don't let life's trials and disappointments
ever steal the Irish from that smile !

They say, quite wisely I think,
That the eyes are the doorway to the soul . . .
And therein lies the truth of what we are, and say, and wish.

W.G. Moon
November 7, 1998
Nashville, Tn

Inspiration for this piece:

Upon my retirement in September 1998, My mother and I took a nice long trip together, by car, across North Carolina and Tennessee. We visited Seabolt family graves in Tennessee, and Lynch family graves in North Carolina. We visited mother's 98 year old childhood nurse, Mamie Lynch, still living with family in Knoxville Tennessee. Then we stayed for three wonderful days at the Opryland Hotel . . . where we had breakfast on the veranda in the atrium, rode the General Jackson Steamer, had our picture taken together there, went to the Grand old Opry show and more. I did my best to spoil her so. We sang the old hymns, and reminised about family as we traveled . . . just we too together. Mom and I cried healthy tears. It was healing; yet as I watched her, I could see that no matter what we did though she clearly loved me and my sister, real life for her had ended when my father died in October 1992. Sadly, I could see it in her eyes. She yearned for the day when she would be with Walter in heaven. She has a good life, with loved ones who show their caring continuously; she's aware that she is well off and she has her faith in God; but "the spark of her day, the cheerleader, organizer who was so constant in her life from the early 1930's is not there. I came away from that trip grateful that we had shared quality time; yet just the same, I felt a sense of sadness that she could not realize the joy of life she still had for her.

Post note:

In October 1999, mother's cancer medicine (She'd had a bout of lymphomic cancer in 1996) failed to block her cancer. It spread to her bones, then to her liver. In January of Year 2000, after serious complications from chemo treatments, she opted to live out her remaining days peacefully. She died March 31,2000. She said she was "ready to go", and that she visualized Walter "standing at the gate of heaven with arms outstretched for her".

To Jeff

If life was a teacup
and you wanted to drink -
I'd fill it with memories
of adventure - love - sharing.

I'd find a way to sweeten it
with something bigger than you and I -
something lasting
to make it all count.

I'd heat it carefully,
taking care to see that it has
just the right aroma before sipping -
then I'd pour it forth vigorously,
taking care to not lose a drop.

Then as you sip it, I'd smile with contentment-
knowing that "I did my best" . . .
knowing that even if its not quite your brew,
you'd know, at least, what I stand for.

W.G. Moon
February 14,1979

Jeff at Hopkins Univ., Baltimore, Md.

Picture of Eileen Lynch Moon

Picture of Jessie Lee Lynch

THE BALLAD OF JESSIE LEE LYNCH

1. In 1919 so the legends been told;
Our heroine had a blessing that was twice unfold.
Said 'ol Able to the Mother don't ya think we've done nice-
Look at that baby . . . and she's come out twice!

CHORUS:

Stylishin', Stylishin'; everybodys' doin' it Stylishin';
Stylishin', Stylishin'; everybodys doin' it -- the Jessie Lee Rag. Bo Bo Bo Boom !

2. Put your hands together; and you hold 'em like that;
bend your wrist completely, make a big top hat.
With your head at an angle, like a real kool kat;
Everybodys doin' it . . . the Jessie Lee Rag !

CHORUS:

3. Slide your right foot forward, do a Tennessee whirl;
Then your step right back; let your hands unfurl.
Bring your hands together; and you hold them like that;
Everybodys doin' it-- the Jessie Lee Rag !

CHORUS:

4. Shake your body all over; Give a GREAT BIG wink;
Put your two hands together, and off you slink.
Give a Jessie Lee WHOOP . . . like a Southern belle dame;
Everybodys doin' it . . . the Jessie Lee Rag !

CHORUS:

W.G. Moon
May, 1994

*a ballad with love from from family at the "150th Birthday" celebration of Eileen Lynch
Moon and Kathleen Lynch Robie.*

Just a Sittin' and a Watchin'

Did ya ever just feel like just. sittin'
And a watchin' ?
Well I do.

I've got the lovliest place to do it in.
It's just a screened porch
In my mountain escape place.

I can see the mountains in the distance
All covered with green and gold
And all sorts of fall colors . . .

I see golphers duffing their balls;
I see deer scampering to get somewhere else;
I see people just out hiking . . .

And talking. yes really talking . . .
Like they ne're find time for back home.
A pleasure to see.

Yes, I can get a real thrill,
Up in the mountains called the Shenandoahs
Just a sittin' and talkin' . . . bout

dreams, and plans, and wishes for tomorrow,
And days gone by, and days to come
Just a sittin, and a watchin'

W.G. Moon
July 2002

You made me feel Like a King

The other day when we talked, I knew you were listening.
The enthusiasm in your manner of speaking
let me know that what I said you thought was important.
Even when we disagreed, you did so in a way
that let me know you loved me.

To differ in our conclusions is no threat
when one realizes that our differences have no impact
on the respect we have for each other.
It's not just father-to-son, or son-to-father . . .
It's person to person.

I am me, and you are thee;
and I thank God for the beauty of both.
I thank you for being honest --
but all the while holding yourself pure to your own values.
Your love has kept us firm.

When you asked for my poems - because they were me - - -
and you found value in them,
you made me feel like a king of my realm - someone of relevance.
You made it known that I was important to your life.
No gift could be dearer.

W.G. Moon
April 10.1981

Inspired by an important telephone conversation with Jay while he was a student at VPI.

THE LAST WORD

I wonder what I would wish to say,
if this day were my last.
Would I want to give you one more hug,
if the die were already cast?

Would I wish for one more tomorrow?
Of course, dear ones. I would.
But the way we loved while I was there,
is the best that I ever could.

I lived each day as though it was,
my very, very best;
and the things I said while I had life,
gives proof to that important test.

I can't think of any instance,
where my love for you e'er waned,
or I doubted that you loved me,
as if that is all that remained.

I haven't stored up things of wealth,
except for one precious thing;
that I loved you dear with all my heart;
with all that comfort brings.

Do not weep for me my darlings.
I've lived each day with zest;
and tell yourself how much I cared;
You were my very best!

And in that bittersweet tomorrow;
when my father gives his urgent call,
think of what we DID together,
as the most important thing of all.

So SING one last great tribute,
to a life that was so full of you;
and my star will shine so vividly,
right down for all to view.

My last word for you who loved me,
would be this final thing;
Love each other as we have loved,
that's the worth of everything!

W.G. Moon
September, 1994

Essay on Life and Death

The Doctor commented that Scott was coming to grips,
for the first time, with the fact that he wasn't immortal !
That's probably the first time in his life
he ever <u>really</u> faced that fact.

I have to admit that, to some extent, I'm to blame for that.
I've always considered myself as somewhat of a superman . . .
that I could do <u>anything</u> I really wanted to do.
I've never ever feared the prospect of dying,
since I came to it close before -when I was a child.

It's strange how such thoughts run through your mind.
I guess - or at least I hope _ we all do that from time to time
- - - taking stock of what we have;
and seeing what we've learned from it all.

Death is inevitable. I don't deny that . . .
but it's not death that we should fear - that's an end in itself-of this physical existence;
but it's only <u>meaninglessness life</u> we should abhor.

What's important to me is that -
each day of life should be significant.
to do otherwise would be a waste of a precious gift.
The chance, if you will, to change things worth changing - - -
or to savor things worth savoring.

Why worry about it; it takes so much away from you.
I say - face whatever it is that lies in front of you,
and turn the day as though it was your last.
It makes a big difference - - - that kind of URGENCY.
If you recognize the reality of death; you can appreciate life.

Immortality, whatever that is, could be a spirit -
a sense of significance - that lives beyond us.
Something like the way we see the light from stars
whose light was emmitted years before our time . . .
and is now only reaching us today.

Think of it,
the light from that star
left it's source before the time of Jesus ___
but it still lives today.
I often reflect on my Grandmother -
Jessie Lee (Seabolt-Lynch) that way.
I'm struck by how much her having been here
has left it's mark - for good and bad -
on those left behind.

She's been dead some fifty years now,
but she's often referred to . . .
and her solid good ol' American basic Christian values -
flavored by early victorian harshness . . . with all it's flaws -
is ever present.

She certainly lives in a prevailing spirit today -
in the lives she touched.
I am reminded by her concern when she gave me the book - Pilgrim's Progress.

The inscription says she hoped that I would take Christian -
a character in the book -
"as my example on how to grow up like a man".
Not bad advice, I think, now . . .
and she had a lot of courage in presenting it to me.

She used to call me "Julius",
after her only - and much revered - son.
He died some twenty years before her.
I always felt special when she did that ___

as though she placed me right up there
with the ones she loved so much;
and it gave me some "living up to do".
Whatever happened to those good ol' days?

Days when people had <u>courage</u>
to live up to a standard for quality -
rather than to show homage to some very temporary,
hedonistic, goal.

Yes, death is a final act ___
in the sense that our physical chance
to change what we stood for can do;
but it's <u>not</u> an end, by any means, if we made that chance count.

Thank God for the chance to live each day more ____
and I'll grab it !
ONE DAY AT A TIME.

W.G. Moon
July,1983

Inspired by a discussion with Scott's Doctor . . . in the emergency room, Hopkins Hospital, on the night Scott (age 17) had to return to the hospital because of infection to his incision 10 days after his open heart surgery . . . an Aortic valve replacement. Unfortunately, Scott had to stay 7 more weeks . . . but, with God's blessing, he survived and went on to a healthy life.

*(WGM) P.S. Maybe that's what dying is for ____
to make sure we (who survive) treasure every moment of life !*

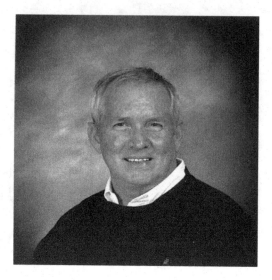

Photo of W.G. Moon about 1986   Photo of W.G. Moon about 2003

A FATHER'S LOVE

Sometimes when I need to feel its all worthwhile,
I stop to think how much you've meant to me . . .
you're love, your laughter,
you're concern for my happiness is evident.

You've pleased me in so many ways, and yet
like any family, we've had times when I wondered -
I wondered if you knew that you were the center of my caring -
as if all else were of lower stature.

But then, as I see you, I see myself in many ways . . .
my good, and my not-so-good.
Forgive me for my shortcomings, but thank you
for your confirmation that all is well with us.

Thank you for understanding that "this hero"
is but a man who tries - - -
that as you grew taller, my smallness was not so disappointing -
that I never lost touch with what you felt important . . .

but instead, we walk together, moving on in your manhood -
building a different, but nicer nest, as best we can . . .
remembering that it's the love we share that binds us ___
not the need to prove who's right.

In time you'll try as I have,
to share your values . . . to make a mark of your own . . .
you'll see, as I have, that it is love and what that brings you
that defines the "bounty" you have sown.

When that day comes when its all over,
and my deeds have all been said,
think of how much I loved you
as those chapters and verse are read.

Think of the good times . . . how we loved and played together.
How we sang, and laughed, and talked.
How we shared ourselves so completely
with no care for what it cost.

Think only of my singing one more "O Lord, how great thou art",
and you'll know my soul is soaring,
stretching toward you as the Lord smiles on approvingly.
Love is the glue that binds all !

W.G. Moon
August 1980

To Luis (AFS Son)

Valentine Day 1979

We share many things with those we like -
to take a walk,
to take a hike.

But stop and "smell the roses"
along the way . . .
that's what it's all about.

A song to sing, a wee bit of caring,
some good old family fun we're sharing.
Yet when it's done -

to remember with thoughts of love those who care -
that, my son, is the secret of living.

W.G. Moon
Valentine Day 2/14/79

Magic Moments -

Inspired by a camping trip with grandson Chaka

Magic moments are those that slip up on you when you least expect it;
And they "steal" the tension and any thoughts of worry and trouble right out of you.

They are times such as a beautiful rainbow sunset right after a late evening storm;
Or that cozy, and comfortable feeling you have just sitting and staring into a campfire.
It might sound a bit corny in a regular setting, but "there are answers to all questions in there."

Some see magic moments just laying out flat discerning the cloud patterns and what you see.
My grandson Jeremy and I did that once. He said he saw "a horsey and a doggie" up there—

I've had wonderful "magic moments" especially when camping out with family.
We've had some really good ones at Nags Head, or Bald Head North Carolina; and some
In Lancaster Pennsylvania I've written about . . . real magic, you can be sure.
I've stored them "in the theatre of my mind" where lots of good things reside.

My attic has many "neat little treasures" I've savored because they connected to a special time.
Some people save sea shells and drift wood, or bottles . . . stuff like that.
I've saved all the many love notes and cards my family has blessed me with.
I've got boxes of news clips and wonderful stuff my unsuspecting "victims" have forgotten—
Like the fort Jeremy and I built to his specifications when he came home from their first mission.

I've got notes, long forgotten, by their master to pop pop Y, saying things like "I just finished
Your grass. Can I get paid?" And one from Scott, home from school one day . . . "whoever finds this, I love you." And I've saved a desk blotter where my 4 year old grandson Chaska left his artwork.I treasure this, and the doodle Emily Grace drew on my pad during a church service years ago. I've got treasures from Josh and Bethany too.

What more can a grateful Pop Pop ever want from life?
I'll never be able to thank Pam for her thoughtful launching these gifts, of life and love.
One time I pulled a rolled-up chalk-drawn "treasure" Scott had drawn in kindergarten.
It was a scene showing a boy and his dog (Scott and Barney) in a snow storm.
Grandma thought we should have it professionally framed; We did, and it still hangs on his son's wall.

Thank God for the blessing of sight and sound to see the art, and hear the music,
And the sayings that people I love have so willingly, and so unknowingly contributed.

WGM June 2012

A Note to My Mom

Dearest Mom,

Just a note to re-emphasize what you mean to my life. It's important - to me - that in our rush to achieve some order of success in our activity that we look backward to our training. Everyone knows that Moms start us in the culture . . . they set the styles, and mores that Dads can only add to. They make <u>all</u> the difference in determining if we will be assertive "self reliants", or dependant "unsures" - gifts we assume from our "first teacher", without notice.

The quality of your love for us all, the depth of your natural talents and personal creativity; and the consistency of your example through the years, has truly stimulated me to reach within . . . but also without.

My cup overflows with the goodness of it all . . . and it would be unjust - of me - if I failed to acknowledge the value of my "great teacher" at whose knee I - literally - learned the meaning of life's major lessons; and who <u>I know</u> will love me for the best, and the least, of what I've done thus far.

I strive to multiply "my inheritance" through the lives of those I touch; so that these values to which I am strongly committed, will increase - and provide a synergy through which this PERFECT LOVE can be felt.

I will <u>always be</u> your loving son . . . and you, <u>my</u> Mom. I thank God for that !

W.G. Moon
Mother's Day May, 1985

Mommy's with her Best friend tonight

Stay away from mommy,
she's with her best friend tonight.

The young boy clung to my coat.
What did I do to deserve such devotion.
He wouldn't let me go,
for more than half the hour.
I'd only been away for two short weeks,
on business . . . my job.

Then I saw how he cowered
when she appeared in the doorway.
His own mother ?
What had happened ?
He later told me,
when we had time alone to talk -

How she had cuffed him
in her drunken anger.
It was in these times
where not even a saint
could say a phrase a-right,
she had her friend with her tonight.

Yet in normal times she'd say
that he was the center of her world;
the most important thing
above all -
the thing she lived for.
then she joined her friend.

It was in those meeting s that
she lost all reference.
the world turned to blur,
all within reach were enemies.
in a fuzzy world.
all except her friend.

From the stein of bitter failure,
and the stench of putrid gas,
she yells out her poison rhetoric,
without a single thought of tomorrows' produce.
It gets worse -
the point of no return.

Oh how we love the person she was,
and hate the act she's in.

the one who could be so swell,
until she sees her friend -
this friend who cares less,
about table hospitality - no tolerance
to share your event or action;
and since I cannot befriend her,

because I'm straight
I'm a rejected "better-than-thou".
a "goody goody" who can't be tolerated
at the party,
and worse -
despised because I can't or won't play.

"mommy hurt me" he said.
"I know" said I",
she'll be alright tomorrow;
but for tonight -
stay away from mommy,
she's with her best friend tonight !"

W.G.Moon
October, 1996

Inspired by a conversation I had with a work friend of mine . . .. Very concerned about his son

Inspired by a real life experience related to me by a friend who suffered because she hurt him, and their son, whenever she was "with her friend". Her "meetings" grew more regular, but she denied the addiction - hell bent to destroy those who share her world. It touched me deeply because of others I'd known whose suffering, though played out differently, was none-the-less to be pitied -- as they threw it all away, for a "friend" who controlled their life so cruel-ly. In day time she somehow pulled it all together; but oh those nightly "meetings" with her best friend.

Picture of Walter M. & Eileen L. Moon

An Ode to Mom and Dad

If anyone asked me if I could choose
between having love and great success,
I'd know without a thought which way I would go -
no second guesses, no second thoughts --
I'd know.

To love and be loved,
that's the secret of life . . .
something to conjure . . . worth the price at any cost;
something to build a life on.
I'd know.

Yes, I'd know because of you,
and what you stand for . . . your actions.
You've given me more than life, and talents, and food,
and brains . . .
You've given me you !

To live with zest,
to make a mark . . . to have a special thing to share -
makes it great to be there, wherever that is --
because you're always in my heart . . .
and that, in my mind, is what it is all about !

W.G. Moon
Valentine Day 1979

Moonstone Glassware Carries a Special Significance to Us

It is DEPRESSION GLASS - this means that it is mature,
and has been around for some time, signifying
a DEGREE OF PERMANENCE and STABILITY -
a characteristic we value in our relationships.

It also reminds us of the GREATNESS THAT GREW OUT OF HARDER DAYS.
These are days that taught us the VALUE OF HUMILITY -
and of the JOY, REWARD and PRIVILEGE of HAVING THE OPPORTUNITY
TO PAY ONE'S OWN WAY,

and through one's own industry; and the double blessing of
having come so far . . .
we can contribute in a meaningful way.
We never want to forget those days !

It's composition is physically hard -
which attests to the POSITIVE ASPECT of it's form;
yet through a variety of designs it demonstrates
how INDIVIDUALITY and UNIQUENESS can exist
though clearly it is a member of the same family.

It's texture is ILLUSIVE;
it's hardness gives way visually to a MOOD OF MISTINESS.
These features blend those principles of TOUGHNESS
and TENDERNESS we recognize as significant
in TRULY GREAT PEOPLE.

Finally --- it's name "MOONSTONE" evokes special feelings . . .
of IDENTITY and SENTIMENTALITY we cherish;
like the GLUE that BINDS US TO EACH OTHER -
reminding us that we embrace the RICHNESS and QUALITY
of all those - past and present - who share the MOON NAMESAKE.

PRESERVING a piece of MOONSTONE GLASS . . .
is to commemorate those values we hold dear !

W.G. Moon
December 9,1983

*Inspired by Carol's request for a simple note about a MOONSTONE
GIFT for Pam and Jay . . . on the occasion of their engagement to be married. The
"task" got out of hand, and grew into this piece;
hopefully, this is broader and more long lasting for all, including Carol to whom I had
already planned to give another Moonstone "family heirloom" at Christmas.*

Dear Mom,

My words are poor communicators of the genuine feelings within my heart.

I am blessed to have a mother who has always, and consistently, <u>taught</u> the lessons of quality living. Such moral guidance is sorely lacking in todays' world.

I am grateful beyond reasonable expression. Grateful for the God given gift of making me your son; not someone else's.

I'm grateful for the creative gifts of art and literature that you and dad delivered me into. I am grateful for the music that you and dad fostered within my being. I often think how far I have been able to go with my music . . . which started with "show me the way to go home."

I am grateful for piano lessons, and cub scout crafts, and even tap dance lessons (though it was awful to me at the time) . . . when it strained the "food money budget".

I am grateful for the example you and dad gave . . . about how people could really love and respect each other year after year, after year . . . when others treated their partnership as a (selfish) temporary experiments at "live in".

Thank you for the sweet echoes in my head. Thank you for the knowledge that you will always be there for me. "Proud of you" no matter what my choices (good and not so good) had led me to. Thank you for being a positive influence in my life, when others operate on a "pity me" theme.

Thank you for being a wonderful mother. I will always work toward (as my dad instructed me) to <u>delight you</u> with the stewardship that love requires. Because you were, and are; I am.

Most of all, I am grateful today, this special day for mothers, that I have you; and you have me (us)! And that I can say to you this day, I love you Mom !!

HAPPY MOTHERS DAY

Love Jerry

There Are Mothers and There Are Mothers

When I look at what you've done -
the kind of loving that goes on around our house,
I see you at every turn,

There are Mothers, and there are Mothers -
but you're the kind of Mother that works overtime
to attend to the smallest of needs . . .
the physical and psychic.

You take the smallest act and make it a party.
You lift us up when we let down on ourselves.
You fill the time with sweetness and caring
that conveys that all is well at home.

Yes, there are Mothers and there are Mothers,
but you're more than just a Mother - - -
you're a wife, a lover . . .
and most of all, you're our BEST FRIEND !

W.G. Moon
May, 1981

Mother's day to Carol

Picture of Carol the one

There's So Much of You Around this Place

Your smile, your grace,
your way of showing your love
is everywhere to see.

I can't pick up an object,
or see a little vase -
that doesn't remind me of
some cherished moment passed.

Your hand print is so clear.
The delicate way you showed
your love so abundantly.

The dash of style,
the sprig of flower;
the remembrance of home
and love, and family . . .

That says I love you
all over again—and again.
There's just so much of you around this place.

And the fragrance lives on
beyond its time.
The dear sweet smell of you,
my lover for eternity !

W.G. Moon
December 3, 2000

Inspired by a shared "honeymoon" weekend at the Opryland Hotel in Nashville Tennessee . . . The beautiful decorations, the excitement of the time . . . and a line that our dear friend Judy Rudolph said to Carol one day - referring to the many personal items Carol had "decorated" her house with over the years.

My Artifacts

The time is coming when I must go—
Tough God knows I'd love to stay longer,
With you, and yours, and all those-
We loved so fully . . . together.

My attic is filled with all
Those collected reminders of love.
They've meant so much to me -
I just couldn't bear to let them go.

Yet now I'm beginning to see
That all we leave behind,
Are just artifacts of a different time
You probably won't even connect with.

Their value, so precious to me,
Is now just a collection of things.
My wife says "get rid of all that";
"It's just junk to those who find it".

But I say, even though that may be true-
Separating from those sweet memories.
Is like being separated from your very soul
And I can't do it !

W.G. Moon
2003

My Day With You

If I could spend a day with anyone in the world,
I'd want it to be with you !
those images pressed so gently in my mind-
Of all we used to do.

Just like precious rose petals; lost, forgotten-
That time has hid from view;
yet when I open that book, in a moment of discovery
Out pops the scent of you.

The times we talked and laughed together-
how we played and walked—and sang.
How you said to me so simply, "you know I'll always love you"-
the prize on which my life of choice to hang.

I chose to see each day more clearly to remind me,
Of the width and depth of you-
and how wonderful it is now to see you blossom,
with the sweetness, yet strength of you.

Oh how proud you've made me, a wealthy man you see-
To think our blood is good and true
And that is why I would choose above all else,
to savor just one more day with thee.

W.G.Moon
May 22,2007

Written to commemorate how Mom and I feel at the blessing of sharing this wonderful
time with each of you—individually, and collectively, as our dear family. It is our deepest
wish that each of us will remember this "magic time together" as the Moon Family,
celebrating our 5oth wedding anniversary on the 49th. You've all been so generous with
us, we wanted to "get the upper hand" this time. We love you dearly !!

Singing on Beauford's bumber

MY QUARTET

My quartet is soft,
Yet oh so strong.
It is a blend of many voices-

No shouting, blaring ends,
We sing the ones recalled
From many prior choices.

We conjure up those thoughts
Of days of life
And oh so sweet amore.

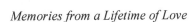

In that old straw hat
With strip-ed vest,
Lilting tunes of days before-

With a bright harmonious que ;
How unified, how blended-
We sing with one accord

Those harmonics keep on ringing
Before the song has ended
The tune lays on the brow.

How wonderful that grand wide gesture
When we bend and smile
And take that final bow.

Walter G. Moon
June 20, 2002

My Grandchildren

I love it when they visit.
I love it when they go.
I 'specially love it in between
When, it seems the action slows.

They run and jump, no stop for breath,
For hours and hours on end.
I wish that I could bottle it -
the en-er-gy they expend

It reminds me now how children act ;
Oh how fast those years have passed—
When I was their daddy's hero,
And now in my repass . . .

I listen as they're singing.
With songs so full of joy;
And if things are ever quiet,
I'd better go to find that boy . . .

Just like it used to be when I was young,
And their dad jumped on top of me.
Now it's their turn to channel all that fun
And I can watch and see

As the roof top does a tremble
And the mess is lying by
And THEY scramble to save a Pop Pop's nerve,
And cure it with a sigh . . .

A sigh that lays so softly
on my now exhausted brow.
we said, "come back real soon, ya hear" . . .
the time for that nap is now !

Inspired by a wonderful family fourth of July weekend at the Woods . . .all three sons,
their beautiful wives . . . and jeremy age 14, Emily age 12, Josh age 7, Pepp age 5 and
Chas age 5. Our crab feast, talent show, fireworks, swimming, golfing, ball game . . . and
more. Never a dull (or quiet) moment. One of those few times when all our family was in
the same country at the same time.

The World through the window of my Values

I wonder why some people see things
as so negative when I tend
to see the same with hope and optimism
about mankind.

I'm talking about our general way
of looking at such things as dealing with people,
how we feel about them - how we work out
life's basic struggles, and the like.

I'm particularly known to convert the word "problems"
into "opportunities".
It's a simple task requiring no effort.
You'd be surprised how well it works for me.

It seems so simple, I wonder why it doesn't
work for others just as well.
But then you have to want something to work -
else all is fruitless. Is that it - - -

The simple matter of wanting something to work so badly
that it, in fact, becomes reality ?
That implies that the act of perception can be quite purposeful
. . . something like, as they say, "having an eye for beauty"

How sad if true; yet I must admit -
those who oppose this view have seemed to have lost
even the most basic patience to try . . . to drift
<u>with</u> the concept before they reject it

as being nothing more than creative delusion,
without substance or support.
Have we come to that - where "beauty" (whatever it is)
has to be <u>proven</u> before we know it - - -

as if all parts can be measured on a scale of 1 to 10;
where music to "satisfy" cannot be free
to come from a different Lyre - - -
I think not !

To be sure, in this age of science and statistics
we've become practical sorts.
But just the same we've lost something
of the spontaneity we've had.

We've scheduled our responses
rather than to have allowed ourselves to flow
with our basic "feel"
for what pleases us.

<u>Two thoughts</u> -

one is that we should be open to it all ---
to see from every view ---
much like a caring parent sees "beauty"
in the handwork of their innocent children;

second, that as we mature,
we should develop opinions we really believe in -
ones that work to carry us forward
no matter what others say.

But it strikes me that in this later point
is the most room for misunderstanding - - -
because even in this confirmed feeling of self satisfaction,
we should listen actively for further insight and guidance.

As we tumble along life's path ---
in a direction affected by prior choices ---
we are touched by other's experiences -
that in themselves, present new directions.

Ah, that's the point.
When we touched, I took the optimists's choice -
you the pessimists' ---
and that has made all the difference ---
in where we each go respectively from here.

W. G. Moon
August 1980

My World Begins With Me

When all seems lost,
and I find myself searching for something to hang onto,
I wonder where it all is.
I ask myself the ultimate question we all wonder about ---
is it me ? Am I the one that's out-of-step,
or am I in uncharted waters where no one holds the key.

I've found that when I look around me at all that's going on -
the fighting, the boozing, the noise of people making action for action' sake.
I wonder.
Is there a pattern in it all that I can learn from ?
Can anyone tell me how to find the peace I'm looking for ?

When you look into "their" eyes, they're empty.
They don't shine back like people who really know what fun is -
the kind of look you see when a person has something to say -
--or wants to hear;
or those who have something, or somebody to go home to.

Then I think about all the good times I've had . . .
those "stolen moments" where I really felt good . . .
and I realize that I had the key all the time.
The feeling starts with me,
and works outward just like those little ripples in a pond.

I think that may be what God meant me to discover;
that, as his created, I must commit myself to action -
not just sit and watch, hoping to gain some reflected wisdom
from people who have but a passing chance of sharing
any serious revealing message to shape my wisdom.

I've had downers, but who hasn't ?
But to think about it, my downers are small
compared to the haunting, empty feeling of loss of a true love,
or when you see someone you love hopelessly ensnared,
for all the wrong reasons . . .

or someone who suffers permanent physical or mental damage.
I'm going to start right now ___ with this very moment.
With Christ's help, I'm going to "gather all my marbles" and take a shot ---
and, if perchance I miss the target today,
well there's always a tomorrow --- to start again.

I'm going to make my own little nest in this world
even if I do go around in circles;
and it'll be me, the real me,
not an empty celluloid image of someone else.
I'm going to collect all sorts of times and experiences.

Not necessarily those kinds that make headlines,
but the kind that make you cry silently . . .
when you remember how deeply you cared . . .
and shared . . .
and how much the experience meant to me.

I'm going to keep on praying -
that everyone will find their own little world -
with their own set of values . . .
the kind you can hang on to because they belong to them alone.
I'm going to wish that everyone can take charge of their own life

. . . not anything great, but adequate to sustain !
But most of all I think I re-learned something today.
I am "chairman of the Board, and President of my own life",
and I'm going to do my best to make my life successful . . .
because now I realize that MY WORLD BEGINS WITH ME !

W.G.Moon
July 1981

Pequay Creek, Pa.
Campground memory

Carol & George Yagle tubing

Jay, Scott, Susan tubing

Dedicated to Susan . . . a friend from Virginia Technic Institute . . . whose conversation and tender listening made me feel that these thought were worth sharing. As repayment, for having shared this, Susan made me a cross stitch wall hanging. I'll hold it as a treasure it forever . . . hearts connected in verse. She "fed back" the words from above "the feeling starts with me, and works outward like those tiny little ripples in a pond".

My Writing

My writing allows me to contemplate my own reality,
to fully explore the real dimensions of my inner soul.
To soar those spots which the sophisticated -disciplined thought
would not allow me to see.

Why ?
because I write what my heart feels -
about life experiences-
and me.

It all comes out of nowhere - and yet deep somewhere
within my inner gratefulness - a kind of recognition,
or cognition, of what the inner me validates.

W.G. Moon
June, 1996

John C. Campbell School
Brasstown, N. Carolina

Now, my Angel (in life) is a full time Angel in heaven

It's O.K. Now, that you've found peace from this terrible disease that caused you to suffer so. Now, all the pain is gone.

I miss you so; though we sensed that the time was near when you'd be leaving. we wished that we were over- reading the signs. Now it is clearer that you knew, God knew, and I even knew, but I hoped for myself that the time we dreaded would wait.
You fought hard for so many years.

The way you did so with such exceptional bravery, dignity and intentional outward denial of your pain and struggle, showed the way God would have us all bear up to our trials in this life. Through it all your love and constant focus was always and totally on family to your last breath.

It hurt me when you whispered through the fog of your final moments . . . "I'm done". I wanted to cry; but I could only sing my love songs to usher you home . . . telling you how much I love you.

Now there's a beautiful new angel in heaven. Go in peace my love.
I promised I'd be O.K. . . .because of you, and because of the love and joys we shared in our extraordinary married life.

W.G. Moon,
November 18, 2012

This piece was inspired by Carol's death November 17, 2012. I scribbled these words while driving home from making arrangement for her celebration service in Wake Forest, N.C.

"Nuttin'"

When you asked me what I made this week,
I'd have to say "oh nuttin' ".

I didn't produce those same kind of finished goods-
as did those blacksmiths,
or those pots of clay the potters made
from their own sweat and care.

I didn't make a painting,
or decorate a doll,
or make a beautiful quilt.

I didn't make a wood carved treasure,
or a basket, or a beautiful lettered piece.
I didn't even enjoy the produce from "Router Magic".

What I did was to search real hard -
for the artifacts around this place.
I wanted to understand what makes the magic
I felt here.

I sense a very special kind of intrigue,
where friendship, joy,
and anticipation -
seem to wait at every turn.

It swells up from the land
where mountain laurel, and honeysuckle,
and dark-eyed daisies sally forth
to meet my waiting eye.

I smelled those rain drenched hay icons
resting there on the meadows rim,
where God kissed them just today.
He meant them for those who will take
the time out to sniff the air.

I heard the sounds of tinkling symbols,
and the hippity hop of string-ed instruments
caressed by loving folk song hands -
right here from Brasstown, N.C.

I saw the smoke rise off the old mountains,
as though drawing the souls of past heros,
of these hills,
ever toward their heavenly home.

Of untold Cherokee Mothers and babes,
torn from these hills for a fatal march to Oklahoma
when Andy gave the word . . .
or the many men who cut the Sorgham . . . or ran the factories
for the gold crop they called "White Lightenin' ".

Well hid - secure as a peg in a shore place -
found only by the distinctive smell ---
just like the smells from a mamas woodstove,
as she cooked the oats for an October morn brood.

I saw the stoplight at Clay's corner.
They say Brasstown is "the possum Capitol of the World",
you know.
I even saw a book there to document
the "flattened Flora and Forna of the North Carolina Hills".

I saw the Murphy Market. They say it's a flea market,
but it had such neat local "lure",
that no self respecting collector of artifacts
could refuse it.

No, I'd have to say that I didn't make nuttin'
this week, but
I learned to turn all those images, and the smells,
and the sounds, and the produce of our hard earned inheritance

from years of preparation - into something very real.
A something that now invades the theater of my mind,
into something of lasting value I wish to share with you today,
and for those who follow us to this mountain place ---
a place well worn by wagon ruts from a thousand Conestoga wagons.

I feel the sacred responsibility
to scratch out this urgent message -
as the circuit riders did in these hills
to tell about the relevancy I sense here
at the John C. Campbell School . . .

a place where all artisans - today and tomorrow -
join with all artists, what'ere their craft -
to stop, smell, hear and carry away a souvenir
of a simpler life and way,

to replant their "earned inheritance"
in other parts of this great land ---
a hybrid, yes, but secure in the honest yearning
for relevant values.

W.G. Moon
June 13,1996
J. Campbell School, N.C.

Aunt Edith's Portrait, about 2003

Ode to Aunt Edie

I've no other friend with whom I've traveled thus far ;
We've covered some four hundred years, and many generations—
To rattle those bones and to have them give up their stories,
Of love—adventure—tears.

You've taught me the joy of ever searching—as a detective would do-
Looking for even the smallest clue about those dear people,
And what they might have seen and felt - -
The passion and excitement they must have sensed as they pressed forward.

Their quest for life, and their ever respect for a benevolent God,
And family, and peace for all.
In my reflections I thank you so for the precious gift we've shared—and how following
your well marked trail has enriched and has given stimulus to my life.

To see the adventure; the need for progress;
The need to press ever forward with an air of confidence and joy—
Our journey has been a looking glass through time;
A glimpse of where in the time machine we've been.

Let's hope that what we started will take root in some great stories to come;
And that what they will do—these heirs of ours whose genes we've shared-
Will make our own walk, our sense of what we've seen and done—
Pale by comparison.

The inspiration for this poem is from the many years my father's sister Edith Moon Wertz
and I searched for family history and genealogy. Edith died September 4, 2007

The Patterns In My Mind

When I'm alone to think,
my mind conjures patterns
of things I love to keep
and share.

my art, my music, my love of life and people around me -
of things aesthetic,
rather than those mundane "building blocks"
we're so used to rambling about.

Most often I'm reminded just how
great it is to be alive;
to see the beauty of HIS handwork,
and how wonderful to have my eyes to see it.

I'm mindful of my "special gift" - - -
an ability to see and be grateful,
than to see with the seemingly insensitive eyes
of those who take it all for granted.

I'm happy to be God's instrument,
to reflect His glory . . . safe in His keeping . . .
to do His bidding -
in whatever way He chooses for me.

I love to sing
for it brings forth a joy of spirit
that surely He meant me to share it . . .
and I feel good !

I love to be with the lonely, the forgotten,
for being there reminds me of His bidding . . .
"unto even the least of these
ye my brethren".

Yea, even in times
when things don't go the way I wish them,
He's there - prodding me onward -
restoring my strength for some future purpose.

I don't know the full meaning God has for me -
certainly not a minister in the theological sense.
But then, He needs, and wants me I am sure,
to minister to his kind; in my own way . . .

and I must go on.
Some day, when the twilight comes, and this life is over,
I know He'll say "come, share your music, your arts,
your zest for having lived with all that's mine . . .

And having tried <u>real hard</u>
to be in harmony with this purpose during my days on earth,
I hope my mark - my having passed by - will live on - - -
in the thoughts and minds of those who knew me.

That they'll say ___ "He was a good man,
a man of honesty and good character ___
a man who knew and loved life for each and every day ___
a father and husband who cared deeply, yet

not too much to smother.
A man who loved God
and worshipped
with his heart".

W.G. Moon
August 1980
Manteo N.C.

"Pinkie Promise"

I "pinkie promise" I'll love you to eternity,
That I'll never forget the way you loved me;
How much you trusted me with your life;
How much we enjoyed life together-

I'll never stop loving the sweet memory of you;
The smell of you;
The taste of you;
The warmth of your sweet embrace.

All those precious thoughts-
Of how you cared for me all those years,
Swirl around my being.
They constantly remind me of the real you . . .

And how very much I loved you always-
For being as lovely and desireable—
As that distant first day when I discovered you.
I "pinkie promise" I'll never let you down.

WGM February 25, 2013

To the girl I met at the Hamilton Rec dance in1954. She
Was 14. We married when she was 19 (1958), and had
The best life anyone could ever dream of.

Carol, my wife, died November 17, 2012.

Scott's Present

What's in a snowflake that makes Scotty run so ?
Whisk - one flake - - then another . . .
and off he goes to the woodpile -
like a "hound on the run".
There's something special about cold wintry days
that sets that boy to runnin'.

I think it's got something to do with love;
or, at least, it seems so - - -
like a mother feels
when she gathers everyone in for a special feast.
I think that's Scott's way of saying . . .
"here, let's get cozy --- here by the fire ".

There's some truth in that, I'm sure.
I feel that way too;
and now I can't help but look for those cozy times
there by "the Franklin'" . . .
listening to the crackle,
with loved ones huddling close.

Have you ever noticed
how everyone backs up to a fireplace ?
Seems peculiar to me - - -
since you get
the least amount of heat
that way.

I'm sure there must be something special
about the peaceful feeling people get
when they stare into fires.
Everybody -who's anybody- does it.
They just look and look - like as if they'll miss something.
But I don't blame them, I like to do it too.

I'll bet ol' Franklin could tell a lot of tales
if he could only talk . . .
about the many times Scott started him 'a talkin' . . .
and about all the love he's seen
around
this place.

Yea, - - - let's get' er goin'-
with one more good old fashion stoker.
We'll share these good times
with you,
and watch
the snow pile up !

W.G. Moon
January 13, 1982

*Scott . . . my ever enthusiastic fan of keeping warm by "ol' Franklin" . . . was age 16
when this was written.*

YA DONE US REAL PROUD

There, right there for all men to see and judge, stands the man;
The man whose roots were set in familiar soil,
whose life stands open to past engagement;
whose life and deed are in naked view.

I remember you, said one; Aren't you the kid that . . .
Hey, aren't you the one who said "I'm going to do it;
I'm going to give my life to God's calling . . .
to do God's bidding" ?

Tell us about what's happened to you. Tell us, did you really go?
Did you really see God's face thru the pain and suffering ones?
Did you really "sell it all and go" as you said you would?
It's been so long since we last talked.

What I now hear, and now see before me is something a parent can only dream for.
A son of pure and giving thought.
Motivated by Gods loving petition to seek what is of real,
not fleeting value.

As I see the man, and remember the boy,
I feel the pride that comes from times we walked and talked;
I see the fruit of the many times a Mom and dad coached the oratory contestant;
the special research writing adventures born out of the excitement of idealistic search.

I know what's behind the speech, and how looking back to what you've shared means
looking forward to the things that you must do;
We who stay behind have a special burden for what you say;
We must lose the very things we cherish most;
God knows how much we care.

God has given so much to us that we must be true at whatever the price;
But, for now, WHAT A MAN! the one who brings such pride from whence he came.
He's the kind of son . . . anyone would want to say "that's MY boy !"
Son, "ya done us real proud".

W.G. Moon
January 27, 1996

*Jay was invited to be speaker about his mission to the Reisterstown Kiwinas Club. I was
privileged to come to say "that's my son, of whom I'm most proud !"*

From the tip of maslow's pyramid

When I got your call the other day, I asked myself "what did you do to deserve all these blessings? "I can count on my one hand the people I know who have had so many wonderful things happen to them.

When you told me that you had just been to a Promise Keepers meeting that day . . . and that one of the men commented that he had just had a blessing. His father had told him he was proud of him . . . and that every man should have that experience *at least once in his life*. You said it reminded you of me, and how many times I've been able to say that . . . how we always end our talks with those kind of exchanges, as though it is the most natural thing to do; and it is . . . at least for us. And I thought as you talked, "yes, that's what your grandpa taught me too". In fact I thought, how blessed we are to be able to say that today. I miss those telephone talks with my Dad - now that he's gone to be with our heavenly father, but I can still hear those words ring true in the back of my head "I'm so proud of you son." It comforted me to reflect that those were the very last words I heard from him just before he died. I've had the pleasure of overhearing you say those very same words to your dear sweet children too. It must be that we *do really harvest the seeds we sow* - - good and not so good.

I'm so lucky to have a son like you, and I know it. Why just the other day I was "bragging" about all the wealth your mom and I've accrued in our lifetimes. We don't claim the material things though we have plenty; in fact you might say we've almost felt pride that the money we spent first was to plant the seeds of true pride and accomplishment in you boys. We are truly wealthy to have seen the beauty of a truly magnificent harvest in God's name. My greatest accomplishment, I tell anyone who will listen, is that I have three grown sons who are ALL well married; and who have brought three such beautiful daughters for us to love and respect. I promptly produce pictures of the many Moons who flow from the security and nurturing of your good parenting. I know you know this, because we've discussed it frequently, but seeing the way you and Pam interact so lovingly and supportively with your little ones and each other, makes us feel good. You've given us so many reasons to see that love in action. Let me count the ways !

How great the view is here atop Maslow's pinnacle; but I can't feel that I got here by myself

I'm here because of you and your brothers and your families. All that your mom and I have done, or tried to do, would be useless if it wasn't for the very thing that money, power or prestige will never buy. I consider the kind of *friendship, love and mutual respect we have for each other as the very most precious thing I have* ! **God has filled our cup to overflowing.**

Thank you son for thinking of me in such a sensative way. I like to think of myself as loving . . . doing as my father . . . earthly (thank God) . . . and heavenly (thank God), would do. Thanks for the urgency to want to share the thoughtful blessing just like you did when you were just a little guy. I'm blessed for the call, and the feeling of being important to your life !

Love, always and abiding . . . *And remember always . . . We're gonna be great ! WGM 1/97*

Reflections

Knowing someone is understanding what's in someone's head.
It's not only listening to what's said . . .
but also to what's intuitive, non verbal language.
It's most important to be in touch,
with what the person's inner voice is saying . . .
like knowing where you've been,
and what those words have triggered before.

It's a source of surprise to me,
to find out that what's been said . . .
is not always what's been heard.
The words go in the same,
but as they swirl around inside that head of yours,
it throws all kinds of switches . . .
some good; some not-so-good.

When we have a little fuss . . .
and I say "let's make up and forget it";
maybe somewhere in your background someone important
said "we'll put it aside for now, but you wait,
I'll bring it up again when you least expect it."
Maybe you never got the chance to feel secure about yourself
because your world "brought you down."

Oh how cruel people can be,
as they take a beautiful spirit, and twist it.
In many ways the world is like the mirrors in a fun house.
When you stand before one you look short and fat;
before another you look tall and skinny;
and yet even another, you look grotesque . . .
while -all the time- the original person looks quite normal.

Would that it were so easy to see - - -
as a twisted piece of glass -
then we'd be able to see it.
We could simply straighten it out all square again.
Maybe the power of real - and honest- love
could do it . . .
if you just had the will to see it.

I wish so that it could be different for you.
I want so much
to share all that's good and decent
from my side of that glass.
It seems so normal to me,
but then, I've had love and decency . . .and respect -
all around me.

You've had so many false starts,
where you wanted and trusted . . .
to only find deception and disappointment.
Is it any wonder you hear and see things differently ?
Come, let us take a new walk together.
Let's put all those ugly symbols behind us now,
and replace them - - -

one at a time . . . with words and deeds of caring;
building new icons of trust, love and acceptance.
I need to let you know I love you now !
and yes, even when we don't always see eye to eye
on every issue -
you need to know that it's alright !
I still care.

W.G. Moon
April, 1982

Inspired by something Carol and Scott were talking about while we were driving overnight to Sanibel Isle Florida

I Remembered

I saw a kid the other day
who looked as guilty as if he'd stolen the Crown Jewels.
You know what, I secretly felt for him though he never knew it;
because I remember a little boy who stole once,
and I remember how very bad I felt when I realized
that I'd let myself and everyone else down.

I felt for that boy because I wonder if he knew
he wasn't so really different -
than other little boys who succumb to worldly temptations.
I wanted to forgive him right then _ _ _
to say "let's talk it out"; but I didn't -
because he'd be too embarrassed to think I <u>even knew.</u>
But . . . I remembered.

I saw a little girl who was so shy
it was as though she was saying . . .
"o go on about what you're doing; don't mind me.
I don't want to be in anybody's way".
she had such a pretty smile . . .
and a nice way about her.

You know, I loved her right then, though she never knew it.
She didn't know that I remembered a shy little boy
who was afraid to talk to girls, and
who wanted to be involved in what they all were doing . . .
but was afraid someone might say "hey kid, get out of here" . . .
Yes, I remembered.

I heard a mother say -
"see, I told you you'd never pick up your clothes",
and I remember thinking why didn't she say -
"I'm disappointed, I thought you'd pick up like you usually do.
You're usually so thoughtful of others" ;
but what came out was so degrading.

I often wonder why everyone thinks
that someone else has all the right answers
instead of themselves.
Isn't it strange - and sad, really -
how people generally seem to feel this way ?

If that little boy, or that little girl, only knew
that they're really not really different from you and me;
or, if that Mom had only stopped to consider that . . .
"all I really meant to say was that I'm just a kid Mom . . .
give me a chance to do what's right before you declare me bad"-
there'd be a world of difference about how I feel about myself.

Feelings are a lot more real than people think.
Everyone of us wants a place to be.
It doesn't have to be so special -
maybe it's just a place to feel secure . . .
and where we don't have to keep proving ourselves again.
I always did say - "you are what you <u>think</u> you are".

Tell a person he's no good enough times, and he'll believe it.
But tell the same boy he's good -
no matter how small the act-
and <u>all kinds</u> of great things happen.
And, you know, it's so easy to do,
you wonder why people don't do it naturally.

You can do anything if you want to enough !
I really believe that.
You can climb a mountain;
you can sing a song;
you can stop to smell the roses;
or you can just stop to share yourself . . .

"Aw, come on" you say . . . but "you're different.
You're a talented person,
a leader, a speaker, a singer, a musician,
a writer of sorts.
It's easy for you to say ".
. . . but I remembered.

I remember how once I stole and how much it troubled me,
and how shy I felt . . . and wondered if I would ever
be strong enough to stand on my own, without support.
I remember how people tried to put me down -
yes, all those things you've felt too - - -
. . . Yes, I remembered.

I see now that the secret to all of life is to keep on trying;
to realize that we're really just human after all.
I now can forgive myself for those little "failures" -
and to try my best now to be my best everyday !
I just wonder now if I can ever tell them - who suffer -
that I remember yesterday; but, oh thank God for today !

W.G. Moon
January, 1982

inspired by a shy little girl who never knew I saw, and noticed . . . and remembered

Jeff preparing & studying

The Roads You Travel

There's a place out there on that long road of life,
where every man finds his niche.
Some sell short for quick reward;
others find an easy spot through luck or chance;
Some go long, to build lives of quality.

It takes real courage to work upstream -
to seek reasons for why it all ticks;
to sift through the offerings;
to find something that fits . . .
rather than settle for hand-me-downs.

I admire that quality you have of getting through the B.S.;
to take it all on the flip flop.
It's so much easier to be taken in by what "they" say is best.
Some see a park bench as a place to rest;
you see it as an office to learn what other viewpoints are.

You're a free spirit, your own man -
the kind who knows how to take it all in;
to listen to every view . . .
you have the courage to decide for yourself what's real for you
- - - and then, go for it !

The quality of your life reflects well on us who love you.
I'm not speaking of your great achievements,
though you've surely done real well in that department -
But it's the quality of what you are, and the roads you travel,
that makes us proud of what you've become.

W.G. Moon
April, 1981

Dedicated to Jeff . . . his induction celebration for Phi Beta Kappa 5-5-81.

The family having fun

It's Times Like This To Savor

Would that I could but just return
to that magic moment we shared,
when the rays of the April Moon
outlined your face and soothed your brow.
How cozy we felt there amidst the Ivy.

The smells of Lilacs; the sounds of a cracklin' fire -
the feel of the balmy breeze with those you love all around;
when time paused in deep respect for all we stood for . . .
where I had you to myself - and no-one else.
It's times like this to savor.

Sing me another song;
a lilting tune about warmth and good times -
a peppy folk song with feeling.
Then lets talk again about what you feel,
and where you're headed. How nice to share those thoughts . . .
with times like these to savor.

Could times be better ? I think not.
It's a magic moment --- the kind that memories are built of.
There's a feeling I have for all this
that tells me to save it . . . to recall the times
when we really communicated what our hearts hold dear . . .

Words are not enough, nor even important -
what counts is that we wanted to be together.
No one could want for more - as we paused there for that time -
to share the knowledge that all is right with us, and would be.
I know you felt it too . . . with times like these to savor.

W.G. Moon
4/20/81

*Dedicated to a special memory of that campfire we all . . . Carol, Jay, Scott and I . . .
shared around the duck pond at VPI in Blacksburg._*

The Lord Will See You Through

What happens to make us feel so small,
to feel so low and restless
when there's so much beauty around us
to be thankful for.

Is it our own SELF-ISH-NESS, our concern for only us _ _ _
or is it that in the midst of our trying day
we only think of the instance, the issue at stake,
rather than focusing on what we, and what our being stands for.

To be sure, there's much good to see in it.
It makes you feel ashamed you've been so fretful.
Why not lift your sights.
Look up to the best, instead of down to the least.
Now you've got it.

Look around you, there's so many ways to see your lot.
The lame, the crippled, the infirmed, have so much less than you.
Yet, have you spent even one moment in giving thanks
for your many blessings ?
I doubt it.

When I feel low, I want to hide;
but that small voice inside me turns me the other way.
It says "go, get off your tail - find a friend who needs you;
Give, give what you've got . . . even if its just your time.
You'll find the peace you're seeking."

It's a formula I've tried many times --- and it works.
But no surprise.
How can one feel sorry for oneself
when you're busy doing for a friend in need.

I <u>know</u> God loves me.
He proves it every day -
and if I can be a Christian in the truest sense ___
yes, that's the answer.

"In Him, and through Him, all gifts are known",
and "by His hand, we are fed".
If we could but just remember those words we'll know that
our life is one of promise, and of Glory - because

We - each in our own way - reflect His light.

Rejoice then, and be glad.
Stop thinking SELF-ish deeds.
Take your real comfort in the Lord.
He will see you through.

W.G. Moon
August, 1980

Sharing

You know, some of the best things happen when you least it.
I try real hard to be thoughtful, but often I feel no one notices—
    Then, zing! Out of nowhere you said
"So many little things turn into big things over time—
    And that's called caring".

That's a score worth keeping - usually just little things—
You said "some poet should capture that in a poem".
    I guess you meant me; so here it is.
I want to keep doing little things to turn them into big things . . .
And hopefully those little things will be what you remember about our life.

                                                  WGM September 2007

Inspired by my life partner and counselor . . .and dear wife . . . Carol

I Feel at Home with the Snyders

Come closer, I've got something to say . . .
about how much you've meant to me this day.
How very important you are;
How much your caring has shown
what beautiful people you are.

You've made me king for a moment,
with all the grace of a gentlemen's gent.
I wonder if you really knew
how much this touched me;
how your having cared has affected my day.

The way you listen; the times we shared;
how interested you were in it all.
You've got a way of loving with all you do
that's so becoming.
I'm so glad that you are my friends.

I feel at home with the Snyders,
they're my kind of folks.
the vision of many times implanted in my brain . . .
of the escapes to the Magothy and Eastern Shore -
we've feasted of the best times where true fellowship,
and all that means, is their nature.

You gave me flowers to brighten my journey.
You gave your ear and comfort.
I thank the Lord that you are my special friends -
and for all the many thoughts of love
that your caring has sent me.

But I thank Him
most of all, for
the time to stop and share,
these important times with the Snyders - - -
the best of all people;
the cream of the crop !

W.G. Moon
October, 1980

Dedicated to our special friends, the Snyders, who made us feel so welcome . . . and who made us feel so welcomed and so loved - each year when we stayed with them on the Magothy . . . and on the Wye River. The flowers on the night table piqued my consciousness, and provoked my awareness . . . of years of sweetest friendship.

A Special Gift

Some folks got it already, and don't know it;
Some wish they could have it, but never will;
Some dream about the time they'll have it,
And then just sit back waiting for their turn
As though it's owed them.

They don't know that it takes a lot of work -
Just to get it, and even more to make it grow.
They have no idea how much effort it takes
To make it healthy, to make it bloom . . .

Or what it feels like once you've arrived;
Or how sweet it tastes on a summer morn,
Or on a cold day by the warming fire . . .
Or on a porch looking out at a sunset in May.

At times there singing by that old piano -
When Daddy sang bass, and Mother sang tenor.
How we beamed the day you went off to school
. . .and when you brought that girl for us to see.

How fast the years fly by, when having fun;
yet how slow the years seemed for one to arrive at 16 . . .
And now that we've got it, it's supreme.
Just knowing it's ours makes it so.

That's what happiness and contentment is all about.
It's the song that starts the day, the hum in your bonnet.
It's the way I see you today, as though it was our first;
And best of all, we've got the gift for living

(Where is) My Someplace

I yearn to find that place out there
where I can have my fill of happiness -
whatever that is.

A place without any bars on the windows,
or where a guy has to do
what everyone say . . . just because.

I don't care about the money -
just so's I can provide what we really need,
and no more.

Seems to me that the price of gettin'
all the frills and such
is just more than I want to pay.

I want my place to be a someplace
for lovin' people, and being loved right back -
because I'm me.

It's not too comfy;
but just someplace I want to go to
because I learn a lot there.

I learn a lot because it's filled with people
who cry a little, sing a little and try a lot;
people who aren't too proud to "let it all out",

and who let me share their load.
My someplace isn't far from here.
It's a neat little place, just because you're there.

It's home base for all sorts of times -
the kind you find when you least expect it.
Like floatin' down the river,

or picking up a batch of wild flowers, just to say "I love you".
Like sittin' and starin' at a campfire together -
as though no one else ever saw it.

It's the prettiest place you ever saw . . .
and it keeps moving around.
everything's "topsy turvy" . . .

like, staking out a piece of ground,
and deciding what goes on inside . . .
then building the walls around "our happening".

It's a retreat of a kind,
but at the same time it's right there in the mainstream
where it all is.

It's my kind of place right here with you.
If you get to my someplace before I do,
won't you give a little yell.

I'll hop right over,
and we'll have some great times . . .
together !

W.G. Moon
August, 1981

MY SOUL NEEDS TO BE FED

To be, or not to be . . . that's what Shakespeare said.
Tis a statement to ponder; But consider this as well.
To live in a state of being only, is what a vegetable does.
What distinguishes us from those inanimate things is spirit . . .
a wholly unpredictable, undefinable, unmeasurable dimension of what we call
humankind.

Loving comes from the soul; but it can only spring forth after it's driven out all thought
of anger and revenge.
My soul can only hold positive thoughts.
It sallies forth in beautiful sunsets, or crisp mountain air-
just like I feel here today in Dinali.
Oh God, why do I fight you so ?

When you love through your soul, you've got to be in condition for it.
It's a feeling that starts at your toes and travels . . . all tingly . . . through your whole
body;
and as it invades you with its' excitement it sometimes mists your eyes as you think of the
many little things you can do to give pieces of its' "produce" to others.

Here's how to feed it.
First, you have to get off somewhere alone where no one will overhear what you are
thinking, except God.
Then, you have to get real quiet and listen . . . listen to the stillness that resides inside
God's wonderful nature.
His sanctuary may be a babbling brook; a bird song; a mountain majestic . . . just like
McKinley before me; or it could be the absolute total stillness of the night.

You know, as I write this I'm reminded how very hard it is to generate words that have
relevance . . . for those times where your soul cries out to be fed;
Because, just like the child we are, we take for granted what we crave the most.
For example, when I said "stillness" of the night.
It struck me that THAT is quite different from the "emptiness" that many people speak
about.
Soul-at-work made the difference.

If only there was some way to fill every busy, routine moment with the same kind of
exciting, love-directed feeling I have as my soul is fed, life would be worth the living all
the more.
I just wonder, is that what heaven is all about ?

W.G. Moon
September, 1994

Mt McKinley, Alaska

THE SPARROWS ON MY SILL

In they flew . . . those unexpected things -
those words so carefully drawn,
like sparrows on my sill,
just standing in wait,
as though paused for -- who knows how long.

feathers, ruffled by the gentle breeze,
seem somehow in need of stroking -
as if to say - "you're there; I'm here;"
but I understand where you are going.

What's in a word anyhow?
A word is not real in itself -
it needs reference; it needs empathy;
it needs human confirmation.

Poetic words are different from just regular words.
They arise from the heart and soul of the event
like the truth unfettered;
like soul . . . shalome.

"Where are you going little one" ? I ask.
as first I smooth his feathers.
Then in response to the warmth he feels,
I wrap my hand around in soft embrace.

But as I feel his beating heart,
I know he must go -
to fly - above - beyond --
to places and things, and people

I'll never see -
but will only know
as his sweet song comes again
from the tree tops on a distant hill.

"There", I said, as I opened my hand -
"fly.
fly my pretty.
Fly on to bring your sweet song back again !"

"Fly on !".

W.G.Moon
March, 1997

*A poem written for my friend Linda - who had the courage to share what she had written
from the depths of her heart . . . about life moving events. Just as the sparrow I wrote
about, her words reminded me about how wonderful it is to trust, and be able to share
through that trusting, things we seldom are willing to let the world of those around us see.
Only poets share such personal experiences . . . sensitively.*

Splash

Have you ever dropped a pebble into a deep well . . .
and waited - but never heard the splash ?
Have you wondered about the classic question . . .
is there a noise when a tree falls in a vacant forest ?

I've often wondered why I felt disappointed
when I shared my poems with others . . .
and received no reaction.
I wondered, until you shared your poems with me -

and now I understand better.
You shared your inner soul -
and as I read, I can see the beauty of your heart and soul.
The sounds of your deepest thoughts come through to me.

You said it all so well, that no one could dare to improve it.
It would be something like having the audacity to
stop a song in mid set.
The mood would be destroyed.

To read your words is to read you -
at rest - in the sanctity of your own "safe place" . . .
to know these were times when you were truly in touch -
with your life, and the things most precious.

What else could one say, except -perhaps-" I love you" . . .
for having treated me to the finest of feasts -
the kind you serve to those you only trust . . .
with your very special china.

Would that everyone had the talent you do,
to give so lovingly.
The world would be a very special place.
I can wish.

You helped me see what others never said.
I read; I drank it in with ravenous thirst;
and when I finished, I felt contented . . .
a warm cozy buzz that tells that all is well.

As I read your words, my heart stretches toward you . . .
to commune with the mood your words created.
To say how much your voice has stirred;
that deepest good we all strive for - - -

to see you- the poet - . . .is to see myself restored.
As you have given, so must I ;
and the silence ? It's something like a prayer . . .
Amen.

Splash!

W.G. Moon
October, 1982

Inspired by the poetry of Pam Alexander - Jay's special girl -
who shared her private poems with me.

STANDS IN LOVE

She stands with majestic poise and purpose
that Indian princess of mine.
Her gaze ever forward,
as though on guard for some far off intruder.

Can you see those distant forebearers ?
Those who traveled the ill-worn paths in basic pursuit -
of food and skins, with children in tow,
a-top her means of travel - a spotted stiff-necked pinto.

That's my precious princess,
who stands firm in her own purposed way -
to support the needs of others in her tribe.
Always . . . she stands in Love !

And for that her tribe has named her -
this beauty whose deep brown eyes reflect so much
. . . about her plains-folk heritage and . . .
of the Dutch and Indian blood she bares

She stands there - firm as a rod before us,
amidst whatever tests may come -
no whimper; no fawning for pity,
she is what she is, this woman who always

stands in love !
How fitting a name she's given -
the one who makes it happen for all her clan.
She stands in quiet, firm devotion to us all.

She says few words about her inner needs and feelings -
but her actions, and those beautiful deep eyes . . .
And the touch of her hand on my sleeve
conveys the message this brave woman-warrior won't say -

Always there, no matter what.
She stoops to help lift a load,
or to say just a word or two
where needed . . .

To make you feel loved . . . and wanted . . .
And needed !
In her stooping, yet still she stands tall,
my princess . . . who . . . stands in love !

Stands in love

W.G. Moon
October, 1996

written for our dear and special daughter-in-love who commented in passing that
"no-one ever wrote a poem for me." I thought then - how could a poet ever miss the
chance to tell her how much she's loved . . . and how she's brought a very special blessing
to our family . . . and our lives.

Sweet Reflections

I want you to remember me,
loving you with all my heart.
Nothing was ever more important
Than these truths right from the start.

There was never a day I meant to miss
any of the words that you might say,
and I can't remember a single time
we spoke harshly before you went away.

I hope that you'll remember,
That as far as I can recall,
You are very much a part of me.
That's the substance of it all.

And in that day of sweet reflection,
Just know that I'll be aware-
That the life I chose to savor,
Was a life with you to share.

W.G. Moon
October 2007

"Teach"

She gave herself to us, that
wonderful woman of words,
whose craft she shared so openly.
Her words were so liberating.

It took the child in me
and gave form, and name, and speed,
to what I had done -
but didn't have the courage to ask

is this poetry?
She showed us that when'er
a soul stretches out
toward distant, beckoning dreams

it's good!
Good to search, and seek,
and smell, and hear,
and feel.

To write is to lift away the cover -
like the gossamer on the bride,
to seek the kiss on that sweet,
dear sweet radiant face.

She freed us to give form
to the thousand precious images
in our minds eye,
where only good things reside.

We will always love her,
as one always remembers the first -
a special, very special feeling
that comes but once

As we taste the bloom --
and speed the harvest.
The teacher starts the engine -
like a bee that flits from place to place,

seldom seeing the produce
of what was started - yet knowing,
yes knowing
that the form that rises

from that flight, born on freedom's wings
is real - and strong - and honest -
and lasting. Oh what a gift
to be a teacher of ideas, dreams and forms

for a million sighs.
God has saved a special reward for her.

W.G. Moon
June 1996

This poem was inspired by my first authentic poetry teacher - Nancy Simpson.

I had written all my life. I had taken the usual English courses in high school and college. I had even written poems for the high school newspaper (Baltimore Polytechnic Institute). I have published newspaper articles in various newspapers in the Baltimore area . . . and in technical magazines and journals (being and engineer); but in time I felt drawn to write in a narrative style emulating my admiration for the words of Robert Frost, Carl Sandberg and others. This form seemed to appeal to the music and the images of the abundant life of experiences stored within my inner place I call the soul in me.

Nancy's poetry, and her words, and her patience, and her special way of showing somehow (I can't even describe it) that she really cared . . . that she really wanted us to see the true art form of poetry, particularly free verse narrative poetry, has given me new insight and inspiration. She showed us that there are many variants on the free verse style to suit particular moods and needs - to free us to communicate within our own selves, and our world.

I had always truly wondered if my writing was idealistic meandering, that if ever exposed to an educated eye would be criticized as unstructured, self serving gibberish. My father, who was an excellent poet of typical rhyme. He never commented on my style. Nancy gave me the gift of naming what my soul felt was right for me. Her encouragement has freed me from my closet space. I now feel worthy to write freely in the style that brings such pleasure . . . and a style that was expressed by many eminent poets in Bill Moyers' book "the language of life".

Thank you Nancy.

Jerry Moon June 1996
p.s.
I wrote this with urgency upon awaking the last day of our time at the John C. Campbell Folk School, Brasstown N.C.
I wanted to give it to our "teach" before we all departed for our various paths.

The Day You Entered My Life

I know I've tried to tell you
In oh so many ways—
That I love you my dear,
And always will,
But this I've just got to say-

The day you entered my life,
Even before you were my new wife
You changed the things
As they were meant to be
and the focus of what
I wished to see
that day you entered my life

I really want to tell you,
How much you've meant to me
how much your constant council
has made a better man of me.
Our life is secure, and that is for sure
because you entered my life.

Wgm 2/1/2007

The Deux Machina Shifts

We all believe that we'll live forever- That is, until suddenly we find out . . . that we've got serious life threatening health issues—Ones that challenge our contented state . . . a major change from what we even dared to believe yesterday.
How did we get here?

Yesterday we had so many dreams . . . things to do; places we wanted to go; important things—even places and stories we wanted so much to share.
Then suddenly, without warning, as though by a curtain call, we step out, to a new audience, where everyone is young, and we are old . . . or "mature' as you used to re-define our condition . . . a new vision that redefines our world, where the role we chose to play in our lives has totally changed.

The Deux Machina shifts, and suddenly more than we ever anticipated, we now for the first time face the reality that life, yes even and especially our own life has limits.
We can't deny, nor now ignore any more, that what we once observed in other's lives, thinking surely we'd have the time to plan for that "someday" out there,
has suddenly . . . and without warning, definitely arrived.
I've always said to everyone that "our lives have been so blessed, beyond anything I've observed in others; that it would be a sin against God to complain".
I meant it; and I still do!

Now I'll have to live up to those words.
I'm grateful, beyond expression for the multitude of rich blessings I've had that tip the balance (of life's scale) toward the light; But I'm shocked, just the same, that the urge I felt just yesterday now seems mired in the present obvious reality that we've seen.

We've shared the best of times -and now, by the grace of God, I'll have to live the rest, best scenes alone . . . brilliantly as you would expect of me.

W. G. Moon, Oct 30, 2012

Inspired by the feelings I had sitting by Carol's side during those long days while she was in a coma state from her cancer at Duke Hospital in Raleigh, NC. Carol, my best friend and wife for 54 exemplary years, died November 17, 2012. The "Deux Machina" refers to the practice in early Greek theatre where the machinery (behind the stage) is activated to change the backdrop of the current scene onstage.

The Miracle on the Air

Someone said that it's a miracle . . .
Because it is hard to imagine
The miracle of transmitting voices
Without wires connected—

To ones we've never seen,
To new friends we'd like to know,
To home-based and mobile stations,
To who knows where.

Yet it happens ---
And because of that we've met,
And talked, and shared.
It's a miracle !

When I stop to think about it . . .
It causes my brain to whirl.
Just think—without the magic of ham radio,
We assembled would never have met.

W.G. Moon 8/2002

Inspired by a visit to the annual picnic of the
Graveyard Net ham operators in NJ . . . a warm
And wonderful bunch of new friends.

The other side of the Moon

We made our pledge that day long ago
laying in that bed of grass- flat out
That whenever there was a full moon,
I'd be on the other side, though we'd be an ocean apart.

I wanted so to bring you comfort
And to let you know how much I care-
Though time and space can separate us
But not from these feeling we share.

I said whenever you see that full bright moon
You'll know I'm standing by-
Though you can't see my face, we can still talk
Don't even question if or why.

We made that pledge that day
So long ago it seems-
And though you've grown and are on your own,
I still watch that moon just to let you know-

I'm here, should you ever need me,
in a cozy place called home.

W.G. Moon
October 2007

Note: This was written to commemorate that day when Jeremy was only about 4 years old . . . getting ready to leave the country with his parents on their mission to Ghana West Africa. I was bringing Jeremy from Virginia Beach to our home in Maryland for one last visit to Grandma and Pop Pop. Without warning, he asked me to pull over to the side and "let's lay down in the grass in the median strip". We did . . . and as we looked up (on our backs that day) we saw a full daytime moon . . . and made our pledge. I don't know if he remembers our pledge; but I do.

The Right Words

I wish I'd said the right things
Each time we disagreed.
"You were right" and "I was wrong"
That's the very words I need.

But in that all-fired up moment,
I tried so hard to subdue,
The need to get- it- right—
to just give my heart to you.

There's no black and white in it,
It's often sort of gray—
But the most important thing in this,
And this I've just got to say . . .

That though I seem to resist it,
I really do admire
The forward bold-strength of you
The way you are on fire.

"Thank you", I say; "please instruct me"
"I'll be a better boy"—
Then things settle down in Ma Ma's house,
Filled with the benefits of joy.

W.G.Moon
October 2007

The stories of my life

My life's a whole bunch of stories . . .
about those things we did together
in those exploring years of our lives

Now-a-days it seems like they flow like a river
at the least prompting.
Remember the time we stayed up all night
to hear the new steerio we bought for Christmas?

Remember how excited we were when our son
gave up his first tooth to an eager tooth fairy . . .
And another time when we oooh-aaahed
at his performance in school ?

When we were there to enjoy the fun of "the Curly Shuffle"
at the hayride - Three Stooge flick with his college pals ?
And when we were" there" the time he just needed to talk.

There's so many situations in life that now bring to mind
the way we reacted to similar instances.
I thank God that we met those events- good and challenging—

And somehow, we did make it through those times, didn't we?
And now we have" wisdom" to share, about how we did it—
And maybe even what we'd do better if we were to do it over.

But wait . . . I wouldn't want that.
I'm delighted with what we produced,
and now I hear "them" tell stories of their own
when we get the families together . . .
even stories about the stories we tell

I thank God that we've shared those times
over all these wonderful years . . .
that what I see in these families is whole and good;
But then, that's another story isn't it ?

W.G. Moon
3-12-2005

The Sun Comes Up In the Morning

Each day brings a new chance to enjoy God's full nature:
To see its potential with all the possibilities you can muster from those sleepy eyes;
And just as surely, God has intended us to see a bright new day.
It is our duty to honor that gift . . . one foot before the other;
One smile, then another and most importantly, a kind word to start the action.

My father used to recite the poem "I know something good about you";
And he'd start each morning revile with the challenge "enthusiasm"!
It's funny how those words, and many other poems dad used to recite
now echo in my mind—a man prone to find beauty and joy amidst whatever life
brought him each day. If I asked him how he was, he'd always say, "GREAT"!

Enthusiasm, just like kindness and a loving nature, can move a mountain of . . . whatever.
I've caught the "bug" from my dad.
I always meet people with the words "another day of challenge and opportunity".
One time I held the door at a major government building for several employees,
And they responded "you must be new around here aren't you"?

Isn't that the way life seems to be these days?
For some reason beyond my understanding, the common person chooses to see things as
Gloom and doom; instead of seeing "possibility" and "opportunity".
It's a mindset; or maybe it's a habit we learned . . . opportunity, or gloom and threatening.
I'm focused on the sun as it rises to welcome a new day, with great opportunities.

How about you?

WGM May 31, 2012

This item was inspired by my happening upon one of my life souvenirs - an aspirin bottle that my secretary at the Rouse Company in Columbia Maryland where I was Program Coordination manager of the New Town project in the mid 1960's, had given me. She had typed the words ""take two when opportunity knocks" and taped it to the bottle. It's been a precious reminder to me all these years . . . a wonderful confirmation that I "broke a twig" as I passed by.

The Gate Van Rensselaer

I get a special feeling at this spot.
There's something here I urge to share with you.
It's the kind of spot you've got to hide from the poets;
or they'll write about it.
You can bet.

It's my special keyhole to the Catskills,
tucked in a tidy special corner at the end of a wall of rocks;
across from the lake, and the trail to the falls.
What a treat for city-folk to see.
Those white birches stand guard till I get back ___

Where gentle hemlocks beacon toward the whispering falls;
the beginning of a quiet adventure . . .
The jumping off point for the spirit of the Catskills.
Surely some romantic soul passed between these portals,
on a moonlit Autumn night.

Where are the people who built these walls so long ago . . .
The signs of some past life filled with hopes and dreams,
that somehow died, or moved on.
They left these remnants for us to see
and feel, and smell, and savor.

This spot is where all the tension you've stored just . . .
oozes out;
and your mind turns to mush.
Where time stands still, for just a time
before you have to move on.

W. G. Moon
November, 1998

Think of the Best Moments of your Life

Close your eyes and float with me if you will.
We can return to the images we had of the best moments of our lives -
Times as sweet as pure honey; smells so fragrant we can almost hear them.
Beautiful flowers of colors—red, blue, yellow and purple- just for the taking.

Imagine with me if you will, the times we took our picnic to Loch Raven Dam -
To "our special tree" where we carved our initials; bet they're still there.
We left them so long ago, as a monument to our young and hopeful love song-
Of times where everything stood still and was filled with dreams we dared wish.

I see the clouds drift overhead, and remember that we saw shapes in them.
We laughed that Linus in the same position saw "a horsey and a doggie.".
We've been treated to it all, and had it all, through all these privileged, bless-ed years;
Life memories that confirmed quality and value . . . days of undiminished intimacy--

Feel the blood flow from your toes through your legs to your body;
Feel the warmth of your beating heart . . . thump, thump, thump—
Now open your eyes and look around at who we are, and what we've become-
Proud and mature factions of what we believed; exalted in all expression of God's Glory

I can live all those joys again, and the many days we've had together, in my minds eye.
My view is just as clear as it was . . .as if we were sharing them from our treasure chest.
Good clean days, some with struggles, but all with a sense of gratefulness, purpose,
And confirmation, that we'd have them to our dying day

It's so wonderful to be able to find a deep sense of contentment, and acceptance,
devoid of negative judgment, or unfilled promises, or to have to say "I'm sorry".
I like us for being just what we are, and where we are.
That's what I think of when I think of the very best moments of our life.

W,G.Moon
November 2008

Picture- Carol in the Surf

Treasure at Nags Head

I saw people laughing today.
Isn't it grand to see their merry smiles,
their sun tanned bodies glistening
as they danced on the sunny shore.

One wave, then another - each with delicate detail -
falls, rolls, and then tethers out
as it finds it's ending point there on the beach . . .
leaving but a small trace of having come.

Then, as if responding to some distant reveille,
it withdraws into the body of the ocean
to play a part - a very different role to be sure -
in some new formation.

There's so much beauty here.
The openness, the harsh yet soft beauty
as far as one can see.
Look, the tiny sandpiper.

See how he seems to dance there . . .
just ahead of each wave ending,
staying just ahead
as it washes the bank of sand.

There, look now. He chases it back into the water,
but always staying a wee bit beyond reach.
It seems like such a silly game - but he plays it once;
then keeps repeating.

As I look upward from the sea
I'm awed by the stark simplicity of this place.
Tho there are many here who share this time,
its not ruined. Its all so peaceful !

See the lonely sea oats that guard the hilltop.
I'm told its their job to guard this place,
lest some anxious storm could claim it.
As they wave so gently, their glistening yellow manes
seem to beacon - to say "come closer;"

"have I got tales I could tell . . . of days long gone,
when Blackbeard used to pass by on his way to hide at Okracoke _ _ _
and even before, When ol' Captain Raleigh came to settle.
I've got a secret to tell about that, but then . . ."

"I've seen ships; O so many ships.
Some came and never left.
Going down to Davy Jones' locker so they said.
But you and I know the real truth. I claimed them for my own."

"Look, I've something for you.
I've saved them just for your coming.
Pretty shells of every type - all washed and cleaned -
just for your delight.

Today is your day, and I thought you'd like them."

There are so many colors to choose from
its hard to know just where to start _ _ _
or perhaps it might be better to know where to stop.
These are enchanting souvenirs

and I'll save them along with my memories of good times
on the banks of Nags Head.

W.G. Moon
August 1980

Outer Banks N.C.

Words Unspoken

I'd like to find the words
to fill the many times I've not said them.
To tell you what you really mean to me
in the scheme of what our life has been.

I honor your opinion.
How what you say affects me.
How much your values pervade our lives,
to make the warmth of "home" within.

I wish I could kiss away each harsh word,
said in times of stress.
In my way, I love you so -
as we strive for our special happiness.

I'd do it again, you know, my love -
as we started it together.
Our boys, our home, our chosen life -
as we stopped to smell the heather.

Until we die, we'll keep it up -
we'll work beside each other;
and lest I fail to tell you so -
you're a good wife, a friend, and mother !

W.G. Moon
Valentine Day February, **1979**

We only have Today

Life is so short in the scheme of world things.
A day, a month, a year - is drawn like the artist's putty
into shapes we never thought were choices,
but in which we shared participation.
How often we just take them for granted, those moments;
Did we use then well, or did we just think they would last forever.

Did we choose words that reflected our honest love,
or did we lose the chance . . . thinking there's always a tomorrow,
amidst the steam of unexpected disappointments and frustrations.
Didn't we realize that nothing stands still, but is in constant
motion towards dying . . . if ever so slowly and un noticed.

Who knows our day in destiny when we must respond to the call,
the day of sweet finality when it's too late to amend or repair.
Heed well this lesson; Run swiftly to the ones you love and value,
Hold them close - and tell them, that *they* are your essence -
It is they who have given you the treasure you value.
Tell themYou will *love them into eternity* !

W.G. Moon
March, 2001

What More Could A Guy Ask For

When I get up to see who I am
I'm grateful for the blessing of life,
And love, and family . . .
And the vision to see good all 'round.

When I think of the misery in so many lives,
Some claimed, some created;
I want to thank God for my abundance-
Freely given, and seldom earned.

I have the very best of all, you see . . .
Sons, daughters, and grandchildren
Who know the meaning of a life of respect
And dedication to preserve love at every turn.

A wife and partner who goes the extra mile
Each day; living as though each were our last;
And friends to share the produce of my joy
Who'll listen as I brag . . .

Not about things, but about values,
And joy filled surprises . . .
About special moments, and mountain top views;
About how you all have pleased me by your attention.

Oh my, how the time does fly,
When a guy has *EVERYTHING* . . .
And a moment to stop and say so.
What more could a guy ask for ?

W.G. Moon
July 2002

What's Really Important In My Life

To share your joys, your disappointments
Your dreams and ambitions . . .
To listen to the excitement in your voice
About your next great adventure.

To see you as you step to meet the challenge
With confidence and surety it will all work,
Even when you don't know how it will-
All go together.

To receive your calls
To be involved in your life . . .
Your questions, and reports . . .
Your reflections about days gone by.

To see myself in your place,
And to know I was there
Some days before,
But never quite as prepared as you are now.

To sing the song of how we've been blessed
And how wonderful it is that this day
Is a day of peace and sharing . . .
With a best and treasured friend.

To feel such pride in all you've done,
And "adventures" yet to come; and yet . . .
To know that because you are,
I will live on beyond my days on earth.

You're my inspiration . . . my hero.
You have made me a wealthy man
In its truest sense.
No one could have ever asked for more !

W.G. Moon 9/12/2002

Dedicated to that special day we shared. I'll be
With you *whenever* . . . and *wherever*

Where Did All the Time Go

If time would just stand still -
So's I could just sit and think,
I'd have the time to see what I've done with my life;
And ponder what I've contributed that's lasting.

I never realized till now,
how important that all seems to me.
I know we'll never live forever—
but we think, and act as we will.

I just realized that what my family is now,
is a true test of what I really valued.
In my unguarded moments, when I was tested;
And, in my better times, when I was rested.

When I look with pride at what you are,
I feel a sense of great satisfaction—
that the stalks are tall and straight;
And I feel so good knowing that you are good people.

Rightly or wrongly, I judge my worth by what you are—
The ones who will carry on when I'm not here;
And when I see the love, and patience, and caring . . .
In the way you act -

I can only hope that this is how you saw me;
And that you felt that I was always there for you—
through your joys, your trials, and your growing.
Oh, where did all that time go?

W.G. Moon
October 10,2003

Wherever You Go

I want to say something to all of you
Who have become a part
Of the fabric of my life.
The color and texture
Which you have brought into my being
Have become a song . . .
And I want to sing it forever.

There is an energy in us
Which makes things happen.
When paths of other persons touch ours,
And we have to be there . . . and let it happen.
When the time of our particular sunset comes—
Our thing, our accomplishment,
Won't really matter a great deal.

But the clarity and care
With which we have loved others
Will speak with sense and sweet vitality
Of the sweet gift of life
We have been for each other

WGMoon 2004

Carol and me in China

WHISPERED LOVE

Did you hear me
When I whispered
How very much
you've meant to me ?

Did you feel it
In your heart
When with a sigh
I wanted you to see

You are the treasure
I always wished for.
The dream my wish
Conveyed.

You're what makes me
Climb that mountain.
You're what calls me
through the day.

Did you hear me
When I whispered
That I love you
More each day - -

Please try to hear it
When I breath it,
That my love is
Here to stay.

Walter G. Moon
June 20, 2002

Inspired by the event of our 44th wedding anniversary (May 31, 1958) . . . and to the one
I've loved and treasured more and more each day

You Made It All Worthwhile

(*to my dearest wife*)

I'm so glad to be here with you today,
to share your thoughts; to spend some time;
to enjoy . . . just for the sake of enjoying . . .
that special gift you have for pleasing.

I don't want to sound corny, but then
what's wrong with just saying . . . "I love you" ?
I think it would be wrong to miss this chance
to just say so . . .

To tell you how happy I am to have been here
with you.

I want you to know that you made it all worthwhile -
that I know that save for what you added,
none of what I did would have been possible.

W.G. Moon
Easter 4/19/81

So Much Hurt for the Wrong Reasons

When you told me that
someone who said they were Christian abused you --
in the name of what the bible said,
my soul cried with you --
Oh, the great deceiver is at work !

How can God's children be left to suffer so ?
The worst of all crimes against God
is to use His name to cover such heinous acts --
and yet -we the faithful- are the victims of Satin's will
unless we keep very close watch.

When man's inhumanity to his kind is done in God's name,
I ask you, can this be His will?
"God so <u>loved</u> the world that he gave His only begotten son,
that whosoever <u>believes in Him</u>
should have life everlasting." (John 3:16)

I ask you would such a loving God ever approve?
A God, who in the form of Jesus Christ
deliberately suffered and died for the sin that is in all of us -
a heinous death of injustice - but necessary
to seal the blood covenant He made with father Abraham.

That in return for loving Him,
all that He is, is ours forever.

Satan, the deceptor, uses the weakest part of God's kingdom -man-to undermine our faith
--
and we are warned about this in the words of Paul
that said "faith, hope and Charity" (love) . . .
"but the greatest of these is charity".

"Love is kind; it is unselfish; it is given in kindness and consideration to the receiver for
their gratification, not ours -
That's the word that Paul gave us.

This poem was inspired by a conversation I had with a young girl who told
me she had been abused by someone who claimed to be a faithful Mason.

SOMEWHERE BETWEEN YESTERDAY AND TOMORROW

As I drift above the clouds in the nowhere between my yesterday reality and the escape I now anticipate,
I am conscious of how fortunate I am to be loved by others . . .
who dispatched us FIRST CLASS.

Seems to me that others just struggle to communicate on the most elementary level;
We, on the other hand, barely need to express a dream, a wish, a desire . . . and loving ones begin to act to make it real!

What a blessing to have such family . . . such loved ones;
The things real life is made of;
A loving son - a loving daughter -- what more could a father or mother ask for ?

You've declared us King and Queen for the day.
It feels so great to be so pampered;
But, as I think back on it, this is not just some special gift for today you've given; it's typical of how you love us all the time!

Dear ones of mine, lest I ever fail to tell you;
I receive your love in my deepest place within me;
the place where the soul searches through the evidence of truth for real meaning;
the place where lies are bared; where truth and only truth resides.

The truth is this --- "Man does not live by bread alone";
He lives, dear ones, in what is true, and love, and sharing.
Your love makes us whole.
That's the truth, and how I measure my worth as a Father.

W.G. Moon
August 28,1994
In the air to Alaska

*note: Written as a thank you to Scott and Vicky . . . for the love gift . . . two first class air
tickets for our Alaska vacation.*
We had the most wonderful of adventures! Their gift made us feel so special.

YOU

When we're apart,
it's your sweet face that draws me home
like the bear which craves to get
at its honey.

You'd think that after all these years
it's a bit obscene to say so -
but it's true,
and I yearn to be with you more than ever.

I yearn for your ever presence beside me -
to give me balance, and correction.
What you cast off means more to me
than all the experts I deal with.

I yearn for your presence,
so I can share the excitement of discovery.
Timing is so important.
Talking to you later is not the same,you know.

Remember how it was when one of our boys
would bring in a daisy, or a June Bug,
or one of those fluffy white Dandy Lion shoots.
Puff, it's gone . . .

or hopped off like the rabbit we see for just
a moment - then scamps away --
and all we can do is call our grandkids and say
"your rabbits back looking for you."

The point is so clear to me - and urgent -
and important to say here today -
because I feel it deep here inside me
where all the wonderful images of you reside.

You ARE more precious to me
than anything I could wish for;
and you are here today. Here --
I'll stroke your face __ and say I love you !

with a heart that lies in your hands -
beating - vulnerable -
anticipating
your every wish.

I yearn to clasp you in my hugging arms,
and kiss your eyes, and ears,
and nose and mouth -
with words of comfort and reassurance,

and if we should ever be parted -
because God calls you home before me . . .
I'll feel the same sweet yearning --
to see your dear face again.

and as you said to me
in passing conversation the other day -
"I hope God saves me the room next to you
in heaven."

What a wonderful thing
for my very best friend to say to me.
"I'll love you into eternity --
and if I get called first
I'll keep the light out for you".

Jerry Moon
June 1996

YOUR WORD (for me)

Your touch is a sweet
Reminder;
Your kiss is something
Even more.

But your word is
Something really special
It's guided many a chore.

But here - -
in my silent reflection,
I see your face so clear
All the more.

You're the dearest friend
To cherish.
my dear
I love you so much more

Walter G. Moon
June 20,2002

Acknowledgements and Copyright information

Various poems in this collection have been included in compilation copyrighted books published by the International Society of Poets (see Poetry.com on the internet; author's name Walter Moon).

While the compilations of the ISP are copyrighted and given a Library of Congress registration number, the copyright for the individual work is the exclusive copyright of the poet. In the following I have summarized most of the poetry thus published and included in various books by the ISP of which I retain the privilege of "Distinguished Member" as VIP P1466I14:

Publication Title	*ISBN*	*W.G.M. Poem*	*See Page*
Tranquil Rains Of Summer 1998	*1-57553-893-8*	*You Made Me Feel Like A King*	*224*
America at the Millennium the Best Poems & Poets of the 20th Century 2000	*1-58235-720X*	*You Made it All Worthwhile*	*29*
A Falling Star 2001	0-7951-5009-1	There's So Much Of You Around This Place	12
Voices From the Soul 2001 Awarded, Editors Choice for Outstanding Achievement of Poetry Dec 2001	0-7951-5057-1	Wherever You Go	24
Waves Of Wonder 2002	0-7951-5066-0	We Only Have Today	33
The Colors of Live 2003 Featured artist recognition	0-7951-5329-6	My Quartet	
The Best Poems & Poets 0f 2003 C 2004 featured artist recognition	-7951-5245-0	Where Did All the Time Go	1
Twighlight Musings Featured artist recognition	application made	I Need You To Know	1
Immortal Verses Series – Winter 2006	pending publication	Echoes of My Father's Love I Need You To Know Inheritance	

My Artifacts

My Quartet

There's So Much Of You

Around this place

To Soothe Your Grieving Heart

We Only Have Today

Where Did All The Time Go

Wherever You Go

You Made it All Worthwhile

You Made Me Feel Like A King

Your Word (for me)

Recent news:

At the invitation of The International Society of Poets, and my nomination to be Poet of the Year 2006, I was invited to read a new poem at the International Society of Poets Annual Convention and Symposium at the Riviera Hotel in Las Vegas July 20-23, 2006. Although I was unable to attend, I was informed I would still be awarded a statuette for Outstanding Achievement in Poetry and commemorative bronze medallion. The Poem I submitted for reading at the convention "In the Pure Joy of The Moment" is included in this book on page 58.

Author Profile Walter G. Moon

Memories from a lifetime of love - "the poetry and writings of WGM"

Random attempts to put down some of the poetry and writings I have felt . . . about people, things, places and events. In so doing I hope to share them with anyone who reads, and to give myself the pleasure of returning to "the theater of my mind" where I might enjoy them again.

In my mind, a man is twice blessed, if he first has the good fortune to see beauty, and second; has the reverence and good manners to return to say "thank you" once the glitter of the first instance has passed.

Supplemental information for background reference:

I have been writing about my life experiences, travels and friendships since very early in my youth . . . discovery of the beauty around me with the eye of a romantic, a poet's eye and ear, an interest in the music of cultures wherever found, and the courage to be a character for those of similar instincts. Have written numerous poetry and local news articles for school papers, and local newspapers, as well as technical articles for national magazines and professional publications. Provided ghost writing support for five technical publications related to Upper Atmosphere Sounding Rockets for NASA . . . numerous technical publications and articles (local papers) for the Randallstown Rocket Society, an Optimist model rockets group. Organized "Wordsmiths" writers group for employees of the Social Security Administration headquarters in Baltimore Md. . . . play scripts, poetry, novelists, songwriters and news releases. Organized a religious Arts Festival for local church to express inter-faith expression of various art forms . . . sculpture, paintings, poetry, prose . . . in the open community. Organized and led several 1-day workshops for Industrial Engineers Association in Effective Technical Communications.

College graduate (engineer) with masters in management. Poem, "You made me feel like a king" was published in the "Tranquil Rains of Summer", National Library of Poetry 1998.Other poems published recently: "There's So Much of You Around This Place", "A Falling Star" 2001, International Library of Poetry; "You Made it All Worthwhile", America at the Millennium, National Library of Poetry, 2000; and several poems . . . "Under a Quicksilver Moon Series", National Library of Poetry, 2002: "There's So Much Of You Around this Place, We only Have Today, Wherever you go, You made it all Worthwhile, You made Me Fell Like a King".

Currently, assembling compilation of my poems for personal collection entitled "Jottings"; and constructing a homepage where poetry will be available to interested friends and family.

Visual-Graphic images related to Poetry—

There's no denying that poetry is an art form to describe the stories, events and impressions that we experience in our lives. Some artists might capture their impressions on canvas, some in well crafted words, some in sounds and music, some through appropriate photography; yet it cannot be denied that visual-graphic images speak loudly and strongly to the poet as he or she encounters the unexpected in everyday living. I've often said that "you've got to be careful what you say around a poet, if it is a poignant, though accidental phrase, it could well be the impetus for a new poem. The same is true of any of the other forms of expression—one sparks the other.

It is with this in mind that I have added the following scrapbook of visual images that relate to the poems in my collection. It is my hope that the photographic image may enhance and explain the narrative, thus bringing my works to an even higher level than could be accomplished without them by further expressing the personalities of the event.

The following index will be of help in that regard:

Poetry Pictures

 —Scott, Jeff and Jay together

 —Carol Francis Zimmerman, My Bride 5-31-58

 —Walter Mitchell Moon, Jerry's Dad

 —Jerry on Way to Africa-

 —Carol on African Trip

 —3 Moon Generations watching the Kite from Deck at Nags Head

 —Kathleen(Lynch) Robie assists as Eileen(Lynch) Moon rubs the gravestone of Laxton Lynch

 —Christ, the Ominipotent Healer

—Eileen L. Moon, shows the 1937 Magazine Cover, and corresponding Rockwell Hummel Figure . . .the frustration she felt as a young mother of 18

—Eileen Lynch Moon smiles her Irish smile

—Jessie Lee Lynch . . . The song describes the antics she and her Husband (Abel Perminter Lynch) acted out for fun. Jerry authored it for Eileen & Kathleen's 150th (twice 75) birthday in 1995

—Walter G. Moon, proud father to Jeffrey A, Walter J., and Michael Scott Moon

—a Picture of W.G. Moon about 2003

—Walter M. Moon & Eileen L.Moon

—Carol Z. Moon captures a landscape in Alaska to share with those back home

—"Singin' at the Bumper" of ol' Beauford

—Aunt Edith (Moon) Wertz—Genealogist, Walter Mitchell Moon's sister

—George Yagle and Carol preparing to launch down ol' Peck

—a- Jay, Scott & school Friend Susan, rolling down the hill into the water of Ol' Peck

 —Jeff at his usual pose, studying for the next big world adventure

 —Jay, Scott and Jerry playing a song " What a Difference you've made in my life" at Eileen & Walt's 60th wedding anniversary party . . .backyard in Reisterstown

 —Carol "hits the surf" at Nags Head. Scott's 4-wheel is in the background . . . ready for the blue fish in the surf

 —Touring China with my sweetie Dec 2004- January 2005. We lodged with Awe & Jeff at their embassy house in Cheng Du China, got to play Santa for an embassy reception toured the country . . . Kunming to The Tiger Leaping Gorge . . . the Great Wall, the Imperial Palace, the Chineese Panda Reserve and more.

THOUGHT ABOUT YOU TODAY

I pulled out my guitar and played a song
not to perform - just because it felt good
to let the music out.
I thought about you today.

I met a stranger who soon became a friend;
we talked and talked, and listened some more,
and shared freely from our hearts.
I thought about you today.

I picked up the kids and rolled on the floor.
We joked and played - just like best friends.
We laughed and hugged - and shed a tear.
I thought about you today.

I encouraged a man who was "down on his luck" -
not to pity him, but to empower him
to help a fellow brother on the road.
I thought about you today.

For you are the one who stamped my life,
as a pattern for me to follow.
Wherever I go, you are always near . . . because
I thought about you today !

W. Jay Moon
6-13-96 (Happy Father's Day)
Brasstown, North Carolina

Isn't it interesting how things turn out. I had "stolen" Jay to take him away for a week at the John C. Campbell School in Brasstown, N.C. I went to take a week of poetry; Jay to work in woodcraft. Would anyone ever expect that HE would be the one who would deliver this beautiful poem. Jay gave me this on father's day. It touched me deeply . . . not only because of his talent, but for the thoughtful words that confirmed that we have arrived where every father dreams to be. I cherish these words as a prize I value more than any other. To be a friend with those you love and care for is about the best of all returns anyone could ever want from investing your dreams, your visions and your values. I felt loved . . . and just as you thought about me today . . . I'll carry those feelings with me into all eternity.